THE HUMORS
& SHAKESPEARE'S
CHARACTERS

JOHN W. DRAPER

Professor of English
West Virginia University

AMS PRESS
NEW YORK

Reprinted with the permission of
Duke University Press

Reprinted from the edition of 1945, Durham
First AMS EDITION published 1965
Second Printing, 1970 ·

International Standard Book Number 0-404-02178-6

Library of Congress Number: 77-142248

AMS PRESS INC.
NEW YORK, N. Y. 10003

THE HUMORS
& SHAKESPEARE'S
CHARACTERS

PREFACE

Since Shakespeare made Hamlet (as the text twice calls him) "melancholy" and made the "fiery" Laertes clearly choleric, since Shakespeare freely uses the terminology of the humors and their associated astral complexions both for passing allusion and for characterizing sundry of his figures, surely, now that three centuries have obscured these old sciences from popular ken, someone should try to fill in this important background of the plays. The present writer, through his interest in Shakespeare's characters as Shakespeare himself and his audience conceived them, has perforce been drawn to the study of this background. After meeting it first in *Hamlet,* he collected bibliography and notes further and further afield, and together with his students published articles written from this point of view on many other characters and plays. Meanwhile, certain of his friends with a kindly-intended optimism, urged on him the composition of a treatise exhausting the whole matter. The present volume has no such ambitious scheme: it undertakes merely to set forth the major aspects of each humor and complexion, with considerable citation of example from the plays and with some analysis of the chief characters concerned. Since much of the material already covered in articles is given here in only an abbreviated form, the reader will forgive the occasional reference to these articles in footnotes. In short, this little study is an introduction to the subject for those who share the author's interest in the characters as Shakespeare (not as some modern) intended them to be interpreted and understood.

The present World War and the untimely death of Professor Frank C. Brown of Duke University have unhappily delayed the publication of this volume; but it seems as pertinent today as it was two or three years ago. My grateful thanks are due to various libraries, especially to the Folger Shake-speare Library and to the Institute of the History of Medicine at the Johns Hopkins University, to Professor H. P. Pettigrew of West Virginia University, to Professor Oliver Elton of Oxford, and also to those friends whose encouragement and good opinion constitute the chief reward that a scholar can expect, above all to Arthur Dayton, Esq., of Charleston, whose kindness has been unfailing.

J. W. D.

May 1, 1944

CONTENTS

THE HUMORS
& SHAKESPEARE'S
CHARACTERS

CHAPTER I

THE HUMORS IN SHAKESPEAREAN INTERPRETATION

With such fine tolerances and niceties of judgment did Shakespeare adjust his plays to the Elizabethan public that, for many years thereafter, no need arose for interpretative comment; and, as long as the language did not greatly change, or the social types and customs that he portrayed, so long no explanation of his plays was necessary for audience or reader. After the Restoration, however, with the passing of several generations and the interruption of the Puritan regime that so profoundly changed the life and outlook of Englishmen, one finds a growth of misunderstanding. Pepys, for example, calls *Twelfth Night* a "silly play," and no longer seems to realize the transition in household life that it depicts[1] nor the Elizabethan feminism that is Olivia's motivating force.[2] Somewhat later, moreover, Rymer's violent strictures on *Othello* and other tragedies show that he quite missed their point; and Dennis, who in 1711 tried to answer him, was likewise far afield.

The eighteenth century was the age of pioneering in Shakespeare scholarship, especially in editing. Theobald was the first who methodically and seriously undertook to establish the text and to explain words and idioms that were no longer current. As the century progressed, the Industrial Revolution in economic life and the rise of democracy in political and social life, together with the concurrent romantic movement in literature and the arts, wrought such great changes that Shakespearean interpretation perforce came into being.

[1] See the present writer, "Olivia's Household," *PMLA*, XLIX, 797 *et seq.*
[2] See the present writer, "The Wooing of Olivia," *Neophil.*, XXIII, 37 *et seq.*

The interpreters, however, were men of letters like Schlegel and Coleridge rather than Elizabethan scholars; and, unconsciously, they endeavored, not so much to set forth the original authentic Shakespeare, as to read into him the ideas and the ideals of their own age: thus they sentimentalized Falstaff, and turned Hamlet into a romantic dreamer. In short, they interpreted, not Shakespeare, but themselves, and used him very much as Wordsworth used rural nature as a symbol and expression of their own thoughts and beliefs. Such a tendency is deeply ingrained in human nature, and appears most amply in the changing interpretations by different races and ages of the Old Testament and the Koran; but of course it falsifies the meaning and defeats the intent of the author. This romantic Shakespearean tradition continued throughout the nineteenth century; and, while meticulous scholars disputed over minutiæ of text and over questions of date and source, most critics and the actors and theatrical producers, unmindful both of the Elizabethan Age and of Shakespeare's meaning and intention, sought mainly for new and striking, rather than authentic, interpretations. The early nineteenth century had bowdlerized Shakespeare; the later nineteenth century Victorianized him. It let its own feelings and predispositions be its guide in determining character and theme: democracy ruined King Claudius; and feminism ruined the passive Ophelia, without restoring the shrewd and independent Olivia; Iago ceased to be a realistic Renaissance petty officer and became an inhuman monster; and most of the plays were so thrown out of focus that critics, though they still repeated the shibboleths about Shakespeare's truth to nature, no longer found in him the illustration of any fundamental truths or principles of conduct, and so could point to no significance or theme. Thus his comedies, without meaning or guiding truth-to-life, became mere farces, and his tragedies, ranting and unmotivated melodrama, sustained only by exquisite, but inappropriate, poetry. So the age largely understood Shakespeare, and so its critics and actors largely depicted him. Indeed, the very priests of the sacred temple reduced their divinity, in their own image, to that of a fourth-rate godlet; and, to the all-important matter of interpretation, the precise historical method given to text and sources was rarely, if ever, systematically applied.

Meanwhile, exact scholars were extending their activities to include the Elizabethan theater, its construction, its business organization, and its stage conventions; and, from this last approach, especially in the hands of Professor Stoll early in the present century, came the first significant broadside against romantic Shakespeare interpretation, which had been running its course through the works of Lamb, Dowden, Professor A. C. Bradley, and the rest. Stoll's results from his study of conventions of character portrayal flatly opposed the accepted romantic interpretations of such major figures as Falstaff and Hamlet; and, though he sometimes overstates the importance of stage convention, a healthy scholarly debate ensued that has spread with the concurrent spread of the scientific method into many aspects of Shakespearean interpretation. The nineteenth century, being a lyric age, had tended to look on Shakespeare's characters as subjective aspects of himself; and now a contrary extreme arose objectifying the plays, and equating his figures with actual Elizabethan individuals, as if, when he drew Shallow he could have had but one stupid justice of the peace in mind. Some critics saw, moreover, a direct relation between certain of the plays and contemporary situations such as the Essex Conspiracy.

It is but a step from specific backgrounds to general; and, during the 1930's, the present writer and his students applied to various plays the background of Elizabethan social and economic conditions and ideals: first, problems of army life as reflected in *Othello* and in *Henry IV,* then the situations of court life of the day as expressed in *As You Like It* and in *Hamlet,* the abuses of contemporary usury as shown in *The Merchant of Venice* and in *Timon of Athens,* the servant problem and the decay of feudal retainers as apparent in the Falstaff plays and in *Twelfth Night;* contemporary law as a background for Ophelia's burial, Desdemona's elopement, and Dogberry's activities as constable; and other aspects of Elizabethan thought and social life were applied to various episodes, situations, and characters, to bring them into focus and to explain, for instance, why Shakespeare approved of a fortune-hunting Bassanio but had no sympathy for Malvolio or Shylock. Political backgrounds also proved significant. At the accession of James I, Shakespeare's company of actors became the "King's Men," directly under royal patronage; and *Macbeth* and *King Lear* reflect the rising interest in political science and especially the theory of Divine Right by which James held the English crown. This political background is linked with Shakespeare's treatment of his sources: why he changed the rule of the legitimate Duncan to make it so good, and blackened that of the usurping Macbeth, why he elevated the characters of Banquo and of Albany because the one was James's ancestor and the other held one of his titles; and James's current struggle to bring Parliamentary union to England and Scotland seems to explain why Shakespeare at just this time presents old Lear's division of his realm with its resultant private and public calamities. So also demonological background threw light on *Hamlet* and *Macbeth,* and the background of marriage law and customs on the problem comedies.

Dramatic characters, however, have not only extraneous relationships with one another but also inner psychological patterns which in a serious and lifelike play, must be complex enough to motivate their various actions in the plot, and must also be integrated, trait by trait, into a convincingly unified personality. In short, characters must be shown not only as *acting* but also as *thinking* and *feeling* as such men on such occasions would think and feel. They must have a true-to-life psychology. Both the Elizabethans and the romantic critics have long agreed that Shakespeare's supreme excellence is his depiction of men and women to the very life; but the critics have hardly bothered to examine into this *very life*—Elizabethans, because it was too close around them to make special investigation necessary; romantic writers, because such a study required long, painstaking research, often in documents difficult of access. Therefore, when the nineteenth century at-

tempted the psychological approach at all, it contented itself
with the psychological theories of its own generation. The
rise of social criticism, however, revealed the need of a more
truly Elizabethan background; but, even before it was under
way, Professor Hardin Craig and his students and Professor
L. B. Campbell and Sir Charles Sherrington had begun to
delve into related Elizabethan science, and, here and there,
applied to Shakespeare's characters the old Galenic system of
humoral psychology, which was still current in that age. Thus
Miss Campbell set forth the "fiery Laertes" as under the influence of choler, and, with some consideration of the humors,
interpreted *Hamlet, Othello, Lear,* and *Macbeth.*

Hamlet's "melancholy" has long formed a major part of
romantic Shakespeare criticism, which made it the keynote of
his character and the explanation of his delay in avenging his
father's murder; this melancholy was the chief difficulty of
those critics who, in opposition to the romantic theory, believed that his delay could be explained on the basis of
common-sense, objective reasons. In 1926 Miss O'Sullivan
brought to light Dr. Timothy Bright's *Treatise on Melancholy*
(1586) and started the serious investigation of Hamlet's psychology in the light of contemporary science; in 1937 the present
writer supported the thesis that melancholy, as the Elizabethans understood it, was not a cause for frustrated action and
delay, but rather a result of these conditions. This study of
melancholy in Hamlet naturally led to the investigation of
other humors in other characters. Corporal Nym is forever
speaking of his "humor": what humor was it? and was it
really his by nature, or was it merely assumed for professional
reasons? Kate and Cassius in Shakespeare's text are called
"choleric"; and Burton in *The Anatomy of Melancholy* cites
Benedick and Beatrice as choleric types: how far are all these
choleric? and in what respects? and does choler explain all of
their somewhat varied actions and characteristics? Dariot says
that Jews are "melancholy": is Shylock melancholy? and, if
so, just how does he show this physical and mental state? The
Duke Orsino in *Twelfth Night* suffers from unrequited love:

does his disease run true to form as shown in Bright, Burton, and other early authorities? and is its sudden cure in the fifth act more medically convincing than it seems to the modern reader?   All these and many similar questions assailed the investigator's mind; and each required (as spare time allowed) careful research and consideration.

Meanwhile, the publication of *A Short Title Catalogue* had made it possible to compile a list of Elizabethan works on popular medicine; the opening of the Huntington Library had made pertinent books available to Professors Craig and Campbell; and the opening of the library of the Johns Hopkins Institute of the History of Medicine and of the Folger Shakespeare Library made it no longer necessary for the present writer to rely on excerpts and summaries made by proxy in the British Museum.   Thus the rare Elizabethan works on medicine, astrology, psychology, and related sciences and pseudo-sciences were made available to American scholars, for the cultivation of this fertile field; and a number of useful books on Elizabethan science have consequently been produced.

Thus by degrees in the present century, the interpretation of Shakespeare's characters has been put on an increasingly substantial basis, especially in the last ten or fifteen years. The crux of drama is character-in-action; and human character has two aspects: its outer relationships between man and man, covered by the social-economic-political approach, and its inner patterns, a matter of psychology which in turn was linked in the Elizabethan mind to the individual's physique, the humor or fluid that dominated his body, and the associated planet, metal, colors, and the rest.   This study will somewhat use the social approach, for it is basic to the psychological; but its chief purpose is to survey a number of Shakespeare's characters from the point of view of the psychological theories and beliefs of the age.   In articles published in medical and other journals here and abroad, some forty characters already have been studied; and perhaps it is time that these scattered materials be brought together in convenient narrow compass so that, with some consideration of yet other characters, the whole may be surveyed, and generalizations perhaps be hazarded on Shakespeare's psychological conceptions and methods of character portrayal.

The Greek mind, as evidenced in its art and its metaphysics, had a passion for system; and, as physical science progressed and data more and more accumulated in Hellenistic and in later times, this Greek passion for schematism took all knowledge for its province, and tried to fit the materials found in the encyclopedic works of Aristotle, Galen, and the rest into a great connected system embracing physiology, psychology, alchemy and astrology, and other fields of contemporary interest. This integration of the sciences, with some inconsistencies where authorities disagreed or parts did not fit, spread from the Classical world into the Moslem Orient, and so through Spain into Mediæval Europe; and thus the Renaissance found it firmly entrenched with such great names as Aristotle and Galen, Rhazes and Avicenna, Bartholomæus Anglicus and Paracelsus, as its authoritative pillars. That Shakespeare read any of these authors is uncertain, though he mentions Aristotle twice and Galen five times; but their theories were both erudite and popular (even Falstaff knew Galen!), and were subject to little serious question until the seventeenth century was well advanced. The common man of necessity encountered this system of pseudo-sciences when (as often happened) he had to dose and diet himself in an age when doctors were few and of dubious repute; and these popular books on medicine, therefore, translated often from French or Latin for the use of the commonalty, seem to have been read so utterly to pieces that few copies remain, and those few often in a fragile state. As Dr. Wright and Professor Craig set forth at some length,[3] they must have been very widely circulated. Warde's translation of Dr. Arcandam's *Booke* required seven printings between the 1560's and 1637; Barrough's *Phisicke* had nine between 1583 and 1637; Batman's revised translation of Bartholomæus had a great vogue; Bright's *Melancholy* had two editions in 1586 and

---

[3] L. B. Wright, *Middle-Class Culture in Elizabethan England* (Chapel Hill, 1935), chap. xv; H. Craig, *Enchanted Glass* (Oxford, 1936), chap. ii.

another in 1613; Cogan's *Hauen of Health* ran through six editions between 1584 and 1636; and others were equally in demand. The tendency, moreover, of Burton, Walkington, and Lemnius in their serious scientific works to cite as examples actual historical characters such as Brutus and Cassius and sometimes even fictional characters such as Benedick and Beatrice, shows that the Elizabethans carried over—as they very naturally would—the same medical and astrological concepts into literature that they were accustomed to in their daily thought, the very theories by which they cured their ailments and calculated lucky times and seasons for embarking on their affairs. The most cogent evidence, however, of the continued popularity of these beliefs is the technical verbiage that they put into permanent use in the language: *influence,* which originally meant the power of the stars over men's lives; *jovial,* which referred to the fortunate and happy influence of the planet Jupiter; *sanguine,* which signified a superfluity of blood and therefore of vitality and good spirits; and so with *mercurial, saturnine, choleric, phlegmatic,* and *melancholy.* Technical terms do not enter common language from sciences that are not common knowledge over a long period.

Shakespeare's many casual references in both plays and poems to the humors and their related astral phenomena are well recognized by lexicography. Schmidt lists thirty-five references to the word *star* as "influencing human fortune" and forty-six to *humor* in the senses of "cast of mind" and "temporary disposition." Malvolio, for example, in his vaulting ambition to marry the Countess, puts his faith in his "starres," his "Fortunes," and the "Fates"; he declares himself of a different "element" from Olivia's other followers; and he thinks that his "complection" should especially commend him to the lady. As Antony's affairs decline, he remarks that his "good Starres . . . Haue left their Orbes, and shot their Fires Into th' Abisme of hell"; and his star, quite properly for a phlegmatic voluptuary, is the "Moone." When all is lost, his "Starre is falne," and "Fortune" has left him. Cleopatra, likewise, refers to "Fortune" repeatedly. Are all these references merely poetic allusion and pretty metaphor? Would they not carry some literal meaning to people who believed in the humors and astral powers and their associated elements, and who, like Queen Elizabeth, engaged astrologers to advise them in their practical affairs? To believe that Shakespeare was beyond his time in this is merely to insist that he was not an Elizabethan, that he did not write in Elizabethan English with Elizabethan concepts, and that he was so incompetent a playwright that he made his text mislead his audience. If, as Professors Lowes and Curry and others have amply shown, Chaucer used astrology and humors for characterization in the *Canterbury Tales,* is it so impossible that Shakespeare likewise did so?

This pseudoscientific system can briefly be summarized. The body has four fluids, or "humors" (compare the Latin *humēre,* to flow or be wet), a preponderance of any one of which affects the physique and the mind in certain recognized ways; and each of these humors is associated with a certain planet, constellation of the zodiac, hours, day, season, colors, metals, diseases, time of life and special situations and events, professions, vocations, and the like. A happy balance of these four humors was supposed to bring mental poise and perfect health, a sort of golden Aristotelian Mean that was surely rare in an age of violence and primitive hygiene. In order to fit the seven planets of astrology into the four humors, the phlegmatic humor was divided into two complexions, respectively under Venus and the moon; and choler, likewise, into two respectively under the influence of Mars and of the sun, which counted as a planet in the Ptolemaic system of astronomy. This took care of six of the planets; the seventh, Mercury, was thought to produce a wavering instability among all four humors. Thus blood (the sanguine humor) was under the power of the planet Jupiter; black bile (melancholy) was under Saturn; phlegm, under Venus or the moon; choler, under Mars or the sun; and a variable nature under Mercury. Blood, moreover, was hot and wet; melancholy, cold and dry; phlegm, cold and wet; and choler, hot and dry. In fitting into this scheme the times of the calendar and of life, the metals,

colors, and so forth, some inconsistency was unavoidable; for
even the ancients did not entirely agree. Lemnius, for instance,
states the matter of bodily colors as follows:

So many being affected or distēpered in their Splene, wombe,
Lyuer, ventricle and Lunges, are commonly either pale, yelow,
tawnie, dunne, duskie, or of some other ill fauoured colour. There
is no surer way (sayth Galene) certainly to knowe the humours and
iuyce in a Creature, then by the colour and outward complexion.
If the body loke very whyte, it is a token yᵗ phlegme in that body,
chiefly reigneth & most aboundeth. If it be pale or yelow, it argueth
that humour to bee greatly Melancholique and Cholerique, and the
bloude to be freshe and reddye: if it be blackish, it betokeneth
blacke adust. Choler, specially if no outwarde accidentall occasion
happed, as great heat or chafing, labour or wearynesse: or if the
mynde bee not intoxicate, and perplexed wyth affectes and passions,
as Angre, Joye, Sorow, Care, pensyuenes: for these make the
humours sometyme to resort unto the skynne & utter parts, and
sometime to hyde and conueyghe themselues farre inwardly: and
for this cause, wee see men yᵗ are fumish and testy to be in a
marueylous heat, proceeding not from any sicknesse or discrasie
but of the motion and stirring of the humours: againe, them that
be affrighted and in mynde amazed, to be pale. Some to loke as
wanne as Lead, some whyte and swartie, sometyme blewishe, sometime of sondrye colours: all which betoken crude humours and raw
iuyce to beare rule and sway in the bodye. . . .[4]

Shakespeare, however, chiefly uses matters of age, profession,
and psychology, which most would concern a playwright;
and, in these respects, contemporary authorities generally agree.

Human life, according to most Elizabethan writers, fell
into three main divisions, childhood, middle age, and senility;
these three might be subdivided into five, seven, or eight parts.
Children and women were properly cold and wet and phlegmatic; old men sank into the debility of melancholy in which
the decline of the vital fluids left them cold and dry; and
middle life was shared according to a variety of theories by
the happy sanguine and the strenuous choleric humors. Of
course, a well-marked humor at birth fixed by the ascendancy

[4] Lemnius, leaves 89 v and 90 r.

of a certain planet, might minimize, or even nullify, these tendencies of age: Sir Toby, though apparently in middle life, seems on the whole to be easygoing and phlegmatic; and Lear, even at eighty, a great age in that day of short life-expectancy, still shows some traces of his innate kingly choler. Particular situations, furthermore, might utterly change the complexion to which one was born: Orsino in *Twelfth Night,* as a young lover and a Duke, should certainly be sanguine, and other characters attribute to him sanguine qualities; but his unrequited passion for Olivia has recently turned his bodily and mental state to the opposite extreme, and lovesickness (as it was supposed to do) has made him melancholy. Thus, time of life, like astral influence at birth, may, or may not, finally determine a character's prevailing humor.

The social status, business, or profession of a figure was also important, if not in causing his humor, at least as a symptom or expression of it. Superficial analogy was still accepted as a sort of proof in scientific thought; and sometimes the adjustment between the four humors, the seven astrological complexions, and the social planes and professional activities was grounded on this obvious but fallacious basis. Sanguine men (as Dariot sets forth) might well, indeed, be nobles, prelates, rich men, and the like; for such high eminence accords in the popular mind with the happiness and good fortune of the sanguine type. Choleric men under Mars should be warriors, brawlers, drunkards, and traitors; but there seems little reason why surgeons and cutlers should be choleric, except that they also use iron cutting implements, and iron was associated with choler. Just why physicians should also be included in this type is difficult to say, unless it was felt that they belonged with surgeons: certainly, Dr. Caius in *Merry Wives* is conceived on this choleric pattern as set forth in Dariot. Choleric persons under the influence of the sun were kings and potentates —and also "laborers of gold," perhaps because, by analogy, gold was considered a royal metal. Women, children, artists, and voluptuaries were phlegmatic under Venus, the soft and pleasing types. Also phlegmatic, but under the moon, which

itself changed and governed the changing tides, were vaga-
bonds, prodigals, queens, sailors, fishermen, servants, and messengers, because of their association with movement or with
water. Phlegm was also, however, thought to be a sluggish
and therefore a stupid humor; thus the astral analogy of the
moon disagrees with the recognized psychology of the type.
The melancholy humor embraces a miscellany of "base trades,"
such as miners, potters, and sink-cleaners; it also includes
husbandmen, Jews (usurers?), Moors, and treasurers: the
humor was under the malefic influence of Saturn, and therefore
would be appropriate to unfortunate or despicable men. One
judges from economic conditions of the age that the life of
treasurer was not regarded as an honorable or a happy one!
How far Shakespeare fitted the social status of his characters
to their several humors is a matter into which the present study
may properly inquire.

For Shakespeare, the psychology of each humor was the
matter of chief importance; fortunately, most authorities on
this aspect were in agreement. A superabundance of the vital
fluid blood gave the sanguine man a handsome body, a happy
outlook on life, and what we moderns would call charm of
personality. He also, however, ran the concomitant risk of
unrequited love which would put him into melancholy, the
worst of all the humors, and also of easy deception and terrible
lusts and passions. The choleric man under Mars was violent,
rash, shameless, or else deceitful and conspiring. The choleric
type under the sun was more like the sanguine but less fortunate. The phlegmatic type under Venus was luxurious, as
befits those given to a life of pleasure: the phlegmatic type
under the moon comprised dolts and fools and cowards (how
does this fit with their being queens, sailors, and historians?).
The melancholy type, like the mercurial, was a cold, dry
humor, and, also like it, ran into extremes: it was most unfortunate and unhealthy; and, in its alternate moodiness and violence, suggests the manic-depressive type in modern psychiatry.
This old Galenic system, however, with all its oddities and inconsistencies, had a certain superficial sense, or it would not, in

slightly variant forms, have dominated science for so many centuries;[5] and sometimes it showed keen medical observation, as when it attributed to red-haired people diseases of the skin. To grasp and to understand all its multiform variations in the Elizabethan consciousness is counsel of perfection; but at least one can master the most obvious and generally held beliefs, and point out their reflection in some Shakespearean characters and passages.

The present study undertakes methodically to survey Shakespeare's use of this complex mass of current theory in his fitting of trait to trait and in his adjustment of a character to its setting and to its necessary actions in the plot. Each astral aspect and each physical and mental characteristic of each of the four humors must be briefly discussed, and one or more examples of Shakespeare's use of it must be rapidly analyzed. Some of the cases by themselves are not quite clear and certain; but every new example that is discovered lends added probability to the whole. Again and again, Shakespeare's own text announces that a character has a "humor," and sometimes even states which one it is; and, from these indubitable examples, one must pass on to those characters whose humor is not precisely mentioned, but who, nevertheless, are consistently portrayed in personality and perhaps also in age and physique and other matters, as belonging to a recognized complexion. Of course, Shakespeare's characters, like people in real life, sometimes assume a humor that they do not have. Sometimes one character mistakes the humor of another, as when Messala attributes the suicide of Cassius to melancholy. Sometimes, moreover, the exigencies of the time unconsciously force on them actions foreign to themselves, as when Cassio's drunkenness augments his choler and makes a brawler of him; and sometimes, through circumstance or age or season of the year, a character evolves from one humor to another, as when Shylock's melancholy, native to a Jew, becomes heated by wrath at Jessica's elopement, and turns to choler. All of these psy-

---

[5] See B. Aschner, "Neo-Hippocratism in Everyday Practice," *Bull. Hist. Med.*, X, 260 *et seq.*

chological situations must be considered: first, the simple humor-characters, such as the sanguine Orlando, the phlegmatic Sir Andrew, and the choleric Hotspur, Laertes, and Iago; then combinations like the perfect balance of health as in Horatio, and mercurial instability as in Richard II and Macbeth; and, finally, the complex figures that assume a humor or that evolve from one humor to another, and so display in their changing personalities the impress of the plot. Such a plan, if circumspectly followed, should constitute an adequate introduction to Shakespeare's use of the humors in his portrayal of character.

CHAPTER II

THE SANGUINE TYPE

The Elizabethan concept of the sanguine type, dominated by the fluid blood, is set forth in a dozen treatises and popular handbooks of the time. These agree in general, though not always in detail; and a composite of their statements should present a fair picture of the Elizabethan concept, which Shakespeare and his audience must have shared. Shakespeare probably knew Batman's popular version of the old encyclopedia by Bartholomæus Anglicus[1] and perhaps also such writers as Dariot and Lemnius; but he does not seem to have followed any single book; and the present study is not concerned with proving his knowledge of one or another of these authors (they have so much in common that this task would be difficult), but rather uses them as an expression of the psycho-medicine popularly current at the time, for out of such popular stuff is drama made. Indeed, Shakespeare's use of the general *corpus* of this doctrine rather than of any one author's theory is borne out by the fact that he reflects the larger matters in which they agree rather than the details in which they sometimes differ. Certainly, as a popular playwright, he could not quite ignore the terms of current popular psychology; and so the pseudo-scientific meanings and the more general implications of these terms must carry over into the plays. Just so, a dramatist today could not use *indigestion, headache,* or *insane* without conveying to his audience the current associations of each of these words.

[1] See L. B. Wright, *Middle-Class Culture in Elizabethan England* (Chapel Hill, N. C., 1935), p. 552; and the present writer, "Jaques' 'Seven Ages,'" *MLN*, LIII, 273-276.

The expression *sanguine* is rare in Shakespeare; but the salient bodily and mental characteristics of the humor are obviously set forth in certain characters. Both physically and astrologically, blood was the best of the bodily fluids; and Elyot explains its physical advantages: "Bloude hath preeminence ouer all other humours in susteinyng of all liuyng creatures, for it hath more conformitie with the oryginall cause of liuyng, by reason of the temperatenesse in heate and moysture, also nourisheth more the body, and restoreth that which is decaied, being the very treasure of lyfe, by losse whereof death immediately foloweth."[2]   Batman,[3] Lemnius,[4] and Walkington[5] agree that the sanguine temper is "the paragon of complexions"; and Cuffe develops the matter at some length: ". . . those of a sanguine constitution are by nature capable of the longest life; as having the two qualities of life best tempred and therefore is compared vnto aire, which is moderately hot and in the highest degree moist. Yet not with that too thinne and fluid waterish moisture, but more oily. . . ."[6]   Cuffe and Dariot associate the sanguine humor with the alchemical element air; and Shakespeare in his forty-fifth sonnet, in *Henry V,* and in *Antony and Cleopatra* contrasts sanguine air and choleric fire with the duller and grosser nature of phlegmatic water and melancholic earth. Ariel, moreover, by his very name, declares his happy sanguine temper.

Again and again, Shakespeare used *blood* as a synonym for *passion;* and this humor properly belongs to his lovers and heroes, particularly those favored by fortune rather than through their own initiative: the King in *Love's Labour's,* Romeo, Bassanio, Fenton in *Merry Wives,* Orlando, Viola and her brother Sebastian, Albany, whose title suggests James 1,[7] Troilus, Florizel, Ferdinand, and Prospero. Its less fortunate side appears in the Senior Duke in *As You Like It,* in Brutus, in Duncan and in the "noble" Edgar and the "credulous" Gloucester in *Lear;* and sometimes, as in Orsino and in Ham-

[2] Elyot (ed. 1541), leaf 8.
[3] Batman (ed. 1582), leaf 30 r.
[4] Lemnius, leaves 86 v and 87 v.
[5] Walkington, p. 111.
[6] Cuffe, pp. 97-98.
[7] See the present writer, "The Occasion of *King Lear,*" *SP,* XXXIV, 181-182.

let, circumstances change a naturally sanguine temper into another humor, and so it loses its happy quality. Sanguine men are generally the favored ones of this world in wealth and social place and especially in youth and charm and success. They often marry beautiful young heiresses; apparently the fathers, who rarely act the part of Capulet, are as delighted as the daughters at the match. In tragedy, this type is rather less common; for it was considered too astrologically fortunate for an evil end, and too static and complacent to have much place in violent tragic action.

Its astrological aspects can rapidly be summarized. According to Dariot, the sanguine man was hot and moist and under the lucky astral influence of Jupiter; blood predominated in his body; the humor was masculine, diurnal, and temperate; and Dariot lists various organs affected such as lungs, ribs, and liver, and various diseases to which the type was subject. He also associates it with "Sweete good odors, Sea-greene or blew, brown, purple, yellow greene, ashe-color," and the metal tin.[8] In *Love's Labour's*, "Samson's love" is described as having a "complexion" that was "sea-water green," for that "is the colour of lovers." Elyot says that blood is most powerful in spring from the ides of March to the ides of May and from the ninth hour of the night to the third in the morning.[9] Lemnius likewise associates it with spring[10] and with the hours from nine to three.[11]

Except for *Romeo and Juliet*, Shakespeare does not seem greatly to use these time elements of judicial astrology. In very few plays are the times of season, month, day, and hour consistently and systematically indicated so that one can perceive, as in Chaucer's *Knight's Tale*, any co-relation of the outcome of each action with the course of the heavenly bodies and with the predominance of their associated humors. *Romeo and Juliet*, however, does show clear traces of an effort to use astrology to give tragic inevitability to the plot. Romeo's meeting Juliet by chance at the Capulet ball is one

[8] Dariot, sig. D 2 v.   [9] Elyot, leaf 71 v.
[10] Lemnius (ed. 1576), leaf 86 v.   [11] Vaughan, p. 126.

of the initial coincidences that have troubled critics, and its ominous significance is indicated beforehand in Romeo's own speech. He fears that they will arrive at the festitivies "too early":

> for my mind misgives
> Some consequence yet hanging in the stars,
> Shall bitterly begin his [its] fearful date
> With this night's revels.

He apparently refers to the fact that the lucky sanguine influence would not be in the ascendant until later at night; and, indeed, their meeting is ultimately unfortunate for both, and they have little chance for private talk until the famous balcony scene, which takes place when it is "almost morning." Most of the misfortunes, moreover, that bring about the catastrophe occur on Tuesday, which was choleric and therefore unlucky; and the lovers die on a mercurial Wednesday before midnight could usher in the fortunate sanguine hours.[12] To fit a plot consistently to astral times and seasons certainly is not easy; but making this astrological motivation clear in the dialogue at each crux of the action, and all in "two hours' traffic of our stage" crowded with action—this is almost impossible. Shakespeare, therefore, was not entirely successful, and never attempted the like again. Perhaps, like Ferrand and Boaystuau, he was becoming a bit skeptical of astrology; or, more probably, his inherent humanity bade him build his dramas on the human mind direct without the interposition of the stars. Perhaps there is astro-dramatic point in his placing *A Midsummer-Night's Dream* and *Twelfth Night* in the sanguine month of May; but no detailed influence of the stars seems evident in the plot structure of these or later plays.

In physique, the sanguine temper was handsome[13] and of "faire stature."[14] Hill describes the type at some length, as having a moderate height, rough skin, moist and soft flesh, and gentle look; the hair lies down, the eyes are fair-sized,

[12] See the present writer, "Shakespeare's 'Star-Crossed Lovers,'" *RES*, XV, 27-30.
[13] Walkington, p. 115; and Arcandam, sig. M 2 r.
[14] Dariot, sig. D 2 v.

the shoulders round and slanting, the voice clear, the palms and fingers long.[15] Vicary and the pseudonymous Dr. Arcandam naturally associate a ruddy color with the humor: if the cheeks "be full, ruddy, and meddled with temperate whiteness, not fat in substance, but meanely fleshly, it betokeneth hotte and moyst compl[e]xion, that is Sanguin and temperate in culler."[16] Lemnius explains bodily color at some length:

> Bloud and vital Spyrite are in their chiefest Pryme and most abound in lusty and flourishing yeares, albeit there is no age y^t lacketh the same: although in ald worne age. bloud begynneth to draw to a coldnes, & the vital spyrit, then neyther so hoate, neither so stronge and effectuous: which thinge as it is in them well to bee obserued and perceyued by their frequente gestures and often moouing of the body and the partes thereof: yet specially maye it be seene & noted by their colour, which in a yonge Stryplyng and youthfull body of good constitution is ruddy and fresh: but in them that be further stryken in yeares, or further of from this temperamente, is not so pure, so beautifull, nor so pleasaunt to behold, for that, all their comelynesse & beauty is eyther faded awaye, or through some euill humours, and hidden imperfection or blemishe appeareth in them worse then in the yonger sort.[17]

All of the sanguine lovers in Shakespeare, from the King of Navarre in *Love's Labour's* to Ferdinand in *The Tempest* are obviously handsome; and Orlando was even a super-champion wrestler. The lover Pyramus in Peter Quince's play must be acted by "a proper man . . . most lovely . . . lily-white" and rose red. Brutus apparently was not of the lean physique that Caesar distrusted; and Duncan, even lying in his gore, was a fine picture of a kindly old man. Orlando's hair, moreover, seems to have been reddish brown; and Phebe apparently regards Rosalind as sanguine, and praises her "complexion" as "red." Shakespeare could rarely use physique for characterization, partly because the writers on physiognomy are inclined to disagree, and partly because any change in casting of the part would create an awkward situation; and, therefore,

[15] Hill, *Schoole,* leaf 7 v.
[16] Arcandam, sig. M 2 r; and Vicary (ed. *EETS*), p. 41.
[17] Lemnius, leaf 89 v.

he is generally content to make his descriptions of the sanguine type merely vague hyperbolic epithets of beauty.

The physiology of the sanguine man—the actual working of the humor in the body—is summarized in medical and astrological works. Vaughan explains: "The sanguine Humor is hot, moist, fatty, sweet, and seated in the liver, because it watereth all the body, and giveth nourishment unto it: out of which likewise issue the naturall spirits. . . ."[18] Lemnius declares the "Lyuer the shop of Blood," and the heart the "fountaine";[19] and Dariot ascribes to the sanguine man diseases of these two organs.[20] This type, moreover, was particularly susceptible to love, which especially affected the heart and liver. As a brief reference to Schmidt's *Lexicon* will show, Shakespeare repeatedly associates these organs with virility in love and in war; and, on the other hand, his compound epithets, *lily-livered, milk-livered, pigeon-livered,* and *white-livered,* imply debility and cowardice. He weaves these concepts, moreover, into the very texture of his characterization. In *Twelfth Night,* the sanguine Duke Orsino, who before the play began had grown melancholy from unrequited love, describes the course of this disease through "Liuer, Braine and Hart"; and elsewhere the comedy touches on this malady to which sanguine persons were so dangerously subject.[21] In general, however, a dramatist is more concerned with the workings of the psychological than with the physical aspects of the human organism, and these physical details in Shakespeare are merely incidental.

The stars and humors were associated not only with certain days and seasons but also with certain periods of life; but authorities show some disagreement as to just what part of middle age—that somewhat indeterminate period between youth and senility—should be considered sanguine. From ancient times, writers had divided human life into three, five, seven, or eight parts; and these divisions had been further

[18] Vaughan, p. 127.   [19] Lemnius, leaf 89 v.
[20] Dariot, sig. D 2 v.
[21] See the present writer, "The Melancholy Duke Orsino," *Bull. Hist. Med.,* IX, 1020 *et seq.*

confused by the varying life-span of different historic periods so that old age might be thought of as commencing anywhere from forty to seventy.[22] Lemnius considers the sanguine humor "proper to lustye flourishing age,"[23] but elsewhere places it in middle life though he calls this period hot and dry.[24] Cuffe associates the humor with summer and therefore with the "Prime" of life from twenty-five to thirty-five or forty;[25] and Dariot, with "flourishing old Age" from sixty to seventy-four.[26] This disagreement of authorities made it difficult to use this aspect of the humor in a play; but by far the majority of Shakespeare's sanguine characters are youthful lovers; and, as Elizabethan men generally contemplated settling down to marriage in their twenties, one judges that in this Shakespeare followed Cuffe rather than Dariot. Albany and Brutus are not really old; and even Duncan need not have been beyond his forties: his sons are clearly quite young men; he is still a hard rider; and if his span of life were nearly out there would have been little point in his assassination.[27] Among the Elizabethans, conditions were unsanitary and disease came early; and so the happy, sanguine time of life should not be placed too late.

Shakespeare as playwright was of course chiefly interested in the psychological aspects of the humors; and blood was replete with admirable traits of character. According to Dariot, it belonged to "honest men, iust, true, beneuolent, liberall, faithfull, milde, godly, shamefast, magnanimous, religious. . . ."[28] Hill ascribes to sanguine men good nature and long memory.[29] Elyot says that they do not nurse a grudge.[30] They are also "moderate, mery, pleasant [witty]";[31] they are "affable in speech" and "liberally minded."[32] Orlando is the perfect exemplar of nearly all these things.[33] He is so mag-

[22] See the present writer, "Jaques' 'Seven Ages,' " MLN, LIII, 273 et seq.; and "The Old Age of King Lear," JEGP, XXXIX, 527 et seq.

[23] Lemnius (ed. 1576), leaf 86 v.　　[24] Ibid. (ed. 1581), leaves 29 v-30.

[25] Cuffe, pp. 118-119.　　[26] Vaughan, p. 121.

[27] See the present writer, "The 'Gracious Duncan,' " MLR, XXXVI, 495 et seq.

[28] Dariot, sig. D 2 v.　　[29] Hill, leaf 7 v.

[30] Elyot, leaf 2 r.　　[31] Arcandam, sig. M 2 r.

[32] Walkington, p. 116.

[33] See the present writer, "Shakespeare's Orlando Inamorato," MLQ, II, 179 et seq.

nanimous and good-natured that he does not bear a grudge against his brother for withholding his inheritance, plotting his death, and forcing him from the paternal roof, and indeed at the conclusion of the play, even after saving him from the lion, does not say a word about restitution. He is faithful in providing for Adam in the forest, though at the risk of his life; he is faithful in his love for Rosalind; and, though exiled, he is merry and bandies repartee. He is called "virtuous" and "gentle, strong and valiant"—truly the beau ideal of chivalry. Very like him is Prince Ferdinand in *The Tempest,* who shows no unseemly terror at the storm, and is led by the magic of Prospero to his good deserts very much as Adam and Rosalind (and good luck) bring Orlando to his. Miranda declares him "A thing divine," and Prospero, more prosaically, "A goodly person"; and the gentleman himself complacently calls himself the "best" of them that speak Italian. Even the harsh business of carrying logs cannot quite damp his spirits, especially with Miranda in the offing. Of course everything turns out well.

The sanguine character, however, had also its weaknesses. Its very superfluity of health made such persons "most giuen to Venus."[34] The devil incited them "to riot, wātonnesse, drunkēnes, wastefulness, prodigality, filthy and detestable loues, horrible lustes. . . ."[35] Coeffeteau declared them "most capable of love" because of the action of the blood upon the liver;[36] and he accused the type of "inconstancy."[37] Walkington declared them "too prone to Venery";[38] and Burton noted that they easily fell into the dangerous complaint of love-melancholy, if their affection was not soon requited.[39] The Romeo of Act I, disconsolately moping because of the cruel Rosaline, is an excellent example of this last;[40] and, as soon as Juliet accepts his love, he rebounds to his natural sanguine humor. Most of these sanguine heroes of Shakespeare are in love, and their love is generally happy in the end; but, in a few instances,

[34] Cogan, sig. Hh 2 v.   [35] Lemnius, leaves 23 v and 101 v.
[36] Coeffeteau, p. 551.   [37] *Ibid.*, p. 238.
[38] Walkington, p. 117.   [39] Burton, Part III, 2, 2, 1.
[40] J. W. Cole, "Romeo and Rosaline," *Neophil.,* XXIV, 285 *et seq.*

all does not turn out so well. With the help of Pandarus, Troilus wins his Cressida, and weds her by common law;[41] but she is ransomed and leaves for the Greek camp, and, being very light o' love, transfers her affections to the valiant Diomedes, who becomes "her knight by proof" in the field of battle; and, at the end, Troilus curses Pandarus. Troilus was merely unfortunate; but Angelo in *Measure for Measure* is highly culpable, and seems to illustrate the vices listed in Coeffeteau as sanguine attributes. He alone of all the persons in Vienna is declared worthy to rule as the Duke's deputy in his absence; he is "A man of stricture and firm abstinence," and starts by strictly enforcing the blue laws long in abeyance; but very soon he himself is attempting the seduction of Isabella, and his unrestrained passions prove his ruin. Perhaps the notorious Lucio[42] is an even more extreme example of a sanguine man sunk in debauchery. Thus sanguine people might, by their very nature, meet serious mischance or even fall to the lowest depths.

In another way also, the sanguine temper was subject to misfortune. Such people were so ideal and so idealistic that their heads were likely to be more in the clouds than on their shoulders; and Walkington mentions them as impractical.[43] Such was the "noble Brutus."[44] His prototype in Plutarch seems to have been partly choleric and partly sanguine; but Shakespeare made him entirely sanguine to contrast with the choleric Cassius. His high character is emphasized over and over, even by his enemy Antony in the final tribute to his memory; indeed, he is "Noble, Wise, Valiant and Honest"; and all the commons, even Antony's own servant, admire his probity. He is so high-minded that at the end he can think of "no man, but he was true to me." Truly, the alchemical "elements" were "So mixt in him, that Nature might stand vp, and say to all the world; This was a man." He is, more-

[41] Hamill Kenny, "Shakespeare's Cressida," *Anglia*, XLIX, 163 *et seq.*
[42] Reginald Lawson, "Lucio in *Measure for Measure*," *Eng. Studies*, XIX, 259 *et seq.*
[43] Walkington, p. 114.
[44] See the present writer, "Cassius and Brutus," *Bull. Hist. Med.*, XIII, 133 *et seq.*

over, in private a loving husband and a kind master to Lucius.
Brutus is clearly sanguine; moreover, he is one of the most
impractical dreamers in all Shakespeare. As Cassius remarks,
his joining the conspiracy runs counter to his own interests;
he foolishly overrides his colleagues in saving Antony's life
and allowing him to speak at Caesar's funeral; he later de-
nounces Cassius in one breath for extorting bribes, and in
the next complains that Cassius had not sent him some of the
money; he insists on advancing to Philippi when a defensive
strategy was wiser; and he loses the battle by ordering the
attack too soon: in politics and war, he is a blunderer. On the
economic plane, the free-handed, sanguine Timon shows himself likewise impractical, for he cannot confine his liberality
within the limits of his purse. Duncan in *Macbeth*[45] and
Gloucester in *Lear* are deliberately tricked to their downfall
by wily villains. Duncan is "gracious" and "meeke"—indeed
"a most sainted king"; but the "constant loving affection"[46] of
the sanguine type makes him a ready victim first of Cawdor
and later of Macbeth. Like Brutus, he is impolitic, trusts himself too readily to his general's hospitality, promises this general every honor, and in the same breath bestows the most
coveted honor, the succession to the Crown, on his own son.
No wonder he is murdered for his pains. Such also is the
perfect Posthumus, to whom each god had given his best, but
who falls to Iachimo's Italian wiles. The sanguine man was
not a shrewd judge of character or affairs, and so might not
end happy and fortunate.

The Galenic scheme of knowledge associated the social
with the physical and the psychological sciences; and certain
occupations and vocations were appropriate to the humor. It
included "Noblemen, Bishops, prelates, Iudges, Lawyers, honest men . . . principalities, &c offices in law, wise in actions,
grave, rich men. . . ."[47] Most of Shakespeare's sanguine men
are nobles or at least great gentlemen, from the King in *Love's
Labour's Lost* to Prince Ferdinand and Duke Prospero. Eliza-

[45] See the present writer, "The 'Gracious Duncan,'" *MLR, cit. sup.*
[46] Walkington, p. 116.   [47] Dariot, sig. D 2 v.

bethan drama wisely avoided the presentation of churchmen, and the men of law play parts too minor to reveal their humors. The most conspicuous example of a "grave, rich man" outside the feudal pale of the nobility is the merchant Antonio; and, at least in the course of the play, he is clearly not sanguine but melancholy, though his "sad" humor seems to arise, not from his innate complexion, but from his momentary worries and the dangers that beset him. In short, most of Shakespeare's clearly sanguine characters come under Dariot's first heading "Noblemen."

The sanguine type is simple, and has no very clear subdivisions; and Shakespeare rather closely follows it in his youthful lovers and heroes. They are marked by a superfluity of blood and by the vitality and virility that should accompany this more abundant life, and with certain corresponding dangers. The astrological aspects of the humor, he uses but little outside *Romeo and Juliet,* where days and hours and astrologic signs more or less govern the episodes. In physique, his sanguine men are, as they should be, strong and handsome: they can wrestle and carry logs and simultaneously make love; and this love affects their hearts and livers according to the best medical belief. They are, quite properly, young, or at least middle aged, and share the prime of life with the choleric humor. They are very Crichtons of charm and elegance, and furthermore, magnanimous and kindly; indeed, Miranda might well declare Ferdinand "divine." When they fall, however, like the angels, it is a sorry fall; and they are especially subject to all the miscarriages of love and to all the misfortunes of an impractical, overtrusting nature. Thus Shakespeare, here or there, has illustrated almost every aspect of the sanguine personality, its fortunate sides in his comedies and romances, its unfortunate in his tragedies, and its vicious lapses in a problem play, *Measure for Measure.* The treatises and handbooks of the age give less space to the sanguine than to the other humors, perhaps because it was considered less complex; and, in Shakespeare also, this simplicity is reflected in the comparative homogeneity of the sanguine persons and also in the fact that he seems to use the humor rather less than he uses the more dramatic melancholy and choleric temperaments; but it is peculiarly appropriate to the heroes of high comedy, realistic or romantic, and it governs the most attractive attributes of some of the most attractive characters in his plays.

Perhaps at this point, one might pause to ask what critical benefit accrues from this approach to Shakespeare's characters. In some cases, as in Chaucer, the association of a planet, or a bodily fluid or organ, or a certain type of stature helps to fix Shakespeare's interpretation of a character. Indeed, the very moment that the handsome Orlando with red-brown hair stepped out upon the stage, the Elizabethans must have known that he was sanguine, and so was doubtless cast as the lover-hero of the comedy; and this expectation gave the plot a psychological motivation and a *vraisemblance* lost on us moderns. Sometimes, furthermore, the knowledge of a character's humor gives his several traits a realistic unity otherwise concealed. Bassanio's sanguine nature, for example, explains Antonio's affection and Portia's love for him, and his for them; it explains the liberality that depleted his former fortunes and the hopefulness with which he embarks on his career of borrowing and wooing: of course, he wins the Casket Test and so the lady; of course, he is generous with Portia's ring; and, of course, he is forgiven and lives happy ever after.[48] Viola in even more parlous straits, shipwrecked without resources, at once wins the Captain's respectful help, goes to the local court, also becomes at once, prime favorite of the Duke, loves, and at last is loved, and so ends a Duchess.[49] Such careers were natural to sanguine people—men with personality, as we say today —for, indeed, they were fortune's minions.

[48] See H. P. Pettigrew, "Bassanio, the Elizabethan Lover," *PQ*, XVI, 296 *et seq.*
[49] See the present writer's *The "Twelfth Night" of Shakespeare's Audience*, about to appear.

CHAPTER III

THE PHLEGMATIC TYPE

The sanguine type was generally so handsome, charming, and admirable in character that one can easily recognize these children of the planet Jupiter; but the phlegmatic type was more passive and less fortunate, and, being divided into two astral complexions respectively under Venus and the moon, it was more diverse and various. It was always, however, cold and moist and either stupid or voluptuous and usually cowardly. Its two extremes are Constable Dogberry and Mark Antony; and it also governed the children and many of the women in Shakespeare. It is generally too passive to precipitate great dramatic crises, but it is often appropriate to comic, and sometimes to romantic, parts. A brief summary of its astral, alchemical, and physiological characteristics may properly introduce a fuller discussion of its psychological traits with some analysis, by way of example, of various pertinent characters in Shakespeare.

Dariot, writing as he does from the astrological point of view, fully distinguishes between the phlegmatic type under the influence of Venus, and that under the influence of the moon. The former, he explains as "temperat, the lesser fortune, fem. of the night, good in all affects . . . ,"[1] and he later adds, "White after some greene, Æthereall, browne glasses of all kinds copper, sweet oyles and fatnes, sweet moist, odoriferous." The phlegm of the moon has less heat and less good fortune; it is "White, green, ashe, yellowe, croceall, pale, siluer & sea-greene, or blewish"; its substances are silver, vitriol, and

[1] Dariot, sig. D 4 r.

salt; and it is of "indifferent fauor, between good and yll."
That phelgm was most powerful in winter and from the third
hour of the evening to the ninth of the night[2] seems to have
significance in *Romeo and Juliet;* for at the ball, which takes
place during these phlegmatic hours, Old Capulet is able to
calm even the fiery Tybalt, who is furious at Romeo's presence.[3]

Vaughan sets forth in brief the function of phlegm in the
body: "The Flegmaticke humour is of colour white, somewhat
brackish like unto sweat, and properly placed in the kidneyes,
which draw unto themselves the water from the bloud, thereby
filling the veines, instead of good pure bloud."[4] Walkington
explains that phlegm thickens the blood,[5] and so the vital powers would be reduced. Elyot discusses "natural" phlegm as
"engendred by insufficēt decoction in the second digestion of
the watry or raw partes of the mattier decoct called Chilus, by
the last digestiõ made apt to be cõuerted into bloud. In this·
humour water hath dominion most principall."[6] Dariot associates phlegm under the influence of Venus with the abdominal
organs, and declares it most subject to "diseases of the stomach
& liuer, and genitall."[7] Phlegm under the influence of the
moon, he associates with the "Brayne, left eye of a man, right
of a woman, stomacke, bellye, left side, stones, bladder, the
members of generation, in a woman the lyuer, tast, brest." He
attributes to it "diseases of those parts" and also "catars or
rhewms palsies, the collick, the menstrues in women, dropsie,
aposthumes, flegnatick, diseases which doe proceed from stop-
ping of the sinews, veynes, falling sicknes, laske or fluxe of
the belly, fluxes of the stomack for want of digestion."[8] Thus
the Prince rightly calls the phlegmatic Falstaff "this swollen
parcel of dropsies"; and in *Troilus,* "catarrhs" are fittingly
linked with venereal disease; and the "rheum" to which
Othello pretends is appropriately "salt." The association of
this humor, furthermore, with the abdominal organs is perhaps

[2] *Ibid.*, sig. E 1 r.
[3] Elyot, leaf 71 v; Lemnius, leaf 86 v; Vaughan, p. 126.
[4] Vaughan, p. 128.   [5] Walkington, chap. xi.
[6] Elyot, leaf 8.   [7] Dariot, sig. D 4 r.
[8] *Ibid.*, sig. E 1.

related to the abdominal distention of Sir Toby Belch and Falstaff.[8a]

In personal appearance, the phlegmatic man, as befitted his sloth, was soft of flesh and usually fat;[9] and "fat," according to Schmidt, meant "heavy and dull": "Fat paunches have lean pates," says Longaville in *Love's Labour's Lost;* and Julius Caesar grew "fat" from the slothful luxuries of Egypt. The cold, moist quality of phlegm, moreover, lacking in vital heat, made the blood slow so that the veins were large; and the phlegmatic man also was either bald, like the apathetic Senators in *Timon,* or had soft hair. Such were the docile courtiers Julius Caesar preferred: men "that are fat, Sleeke-headed men, and such as sleepe a-nights." Such presumably was the "fat" cook in *A Comedy of Errors,* "the fat ale-wife of Wincot" in *The Taming of the Shrew,* the "fat and greasy citizens" mentioned by Jaques and his pompous justice, mouthing bland truisms, "In fair round belly with good capon lined." Such is Sir Toby, who scouts the notion that his clothes should "confine" his girth any "finer." Such is Dogberry, towering in his pride of place, surveying himself and declaring that he is "as pretty a piece of flesh as any in Messina." Such, above all others, is "fat Falstaff," whose architectural amplitude is emphasized by his tiny page. Mistress Ford proposes to slenderize this bulk by burning it down with the sanguine heat of seeming-requited love: "I think the best way were to entertain him with hope, till the wicked fire of lust have melted him in his own grease."

On the other hand, the sluggishness of phlegm implied stupidity; and men "dull of capacity" were thought to have tall bodies and long, thin legs:[10] such a "clodde-pole" is the "tall" Sir Andrew, who has been called the stupidest gull in all drama. Such also, in build and mental caliber are Slender, with his "little wee face" and "little yellow beard," who cannot converse without his book of jokes, and also his uncle

---

[8a] Falstaff's physical infirmity may well have coincided with that of the actor Pope, for whom the part was written. See the present writer, "Speech-Tempo in Shylock," *JEGP,* about to appear.

[9] Elyot, leaf 2 v; and Batman, leaf 32 r.   [10] Hill, leaves 110, 210, and 123 v.

Shallow,[11] whose boasts of his youthful exploits contrasting with his skinniness roused Falstaff's taunts. The Elizabethans believed in the Golden Mean of Aristotle; and phlegm, when satirized, is commonly displayed in one of these physical extremes: the grandiose waddle of Falstaff, or Sir Andrew's broomstick legs skipping about in a drunken dance, or stout Sir Toby ogling his "youngest wren," Maria. Such extremes are the very stuff of caricature; but, to the Elizabethans, they carried also psychological implications lost on the modern reader: a Falstaff, so enormously rotund and therefore so phlegmatic, could not to Shakespeare's audience have been the fine and valiant soldier that Professor Bradley thinks him, and the fat knight's ridicule of Shallow's wizened frame and empty boasts recoils against himself; for he also shared in the humor that occasioned it.

Sir Andrew is one of the few characters in Shakespeare whose physique is rather fully set forth in the text; and every detail points, if not directly to his phlegmatic humor, at least to the stupidity that was its *alter ego*. He is, like Slender, a "thin-fac'd knaue"; and a high or long forehead implied "dull witte," and also "unshamefastnesse" and impudence.[12] Certainly, his continued lingering, uninvited, in the household of the Countess, when she would not even receive him, suggests no great fineness of feeling on his part. Perhaps the gawky knight should also be made up to accord with the "obliquity or crookedness of countenance" that Dariot attributes to lunar phlegm.[13] Sir Andrew's hair, furthermore, "hangs like flax on a distaffe"; and "hair right downward" was the sign of "simple" men.[14] The comparison to flax suggests that it was of a pale color; and such colors, especially of the hair, belonged to phlegm.[15] Lemnius says that "Persōs Phlegmatick" are ill colored, pale, and (like Slender) thin of hair.[16] The pseudon-

[11] See the present writer, "Robert Shallow Esq., J. P.," *Neuphil. Mitt.*, XXXVIII, 257 *et seq.*

[12] Arcandam, appended "Phisiognomie"; Hill, leaves 28 and 32 v.

[13] Dariot, sig. E 1 r.

[14] Arcandam, "Phisiognomie"; Hill, leaf 10 v.

[15] Vicary, p. 41; Dariot, sig. E 1 r; Vaughan, p. 128.

[16] Lemnius, leaf 146 r.

ymous Dr. Arcandam associates a "meane color" with bold-
ness and strength, but takes the extremes of pale, white and
black as implying cowardice.[17]   In *Antony and Cleopatra*,
after the disgraceful flight from the Battle of Actium, Antony
cries out:

> My very haires do mutiny: for the white
> Reprove the browne for rashnesse, and they them
> For feare, and doting.

According to Dariot, both brown and white were phlegmatic
colors;[18] but white especially stood for cowardice. Indeed, as
Schmidt's *Lexicon* shows, such terms as *white* and *milk-livered*
in Shakespeare have a craven connotation.

Cowardice, stupidity, and sloth, the bad qualities of the
phlegmatic humor, appear least in women and children, who
were of this complexion by virtue of their sex or age. Cowardice in them is surely to be forgiven; and, on the supreme
authority of Aristotle, moreover, Hill declares that cold and
moist individuals "verye small of personage" are "apt to con-
ceyue and readily to decerne."[19]   A small body gave a ready
wit[20] and made one "Wise";[21] and so these women and children were often far from stupid. This would explain the
difference between the lanky dolt Sir Andrew and the dimin-
utive and shrewd Maria; both are phlegmatic but an utter
contrast in both stature and intelligence. For like reason, the
children in Shakespeare, most of whom should be phlegmatic,
are nevertheless both attractive and alert. Brutus' page Lucius
has a sweet and yielding nature, is a musician and sleeps easily,
and so accords with the phlegmatic type; but what we see of
him and of his master's affection for him does not suggest that
he is anyone's fool. Falstaff's unfortunate page Robin grows
sly and clever with years and hard experience;[22] and Prince
Arthur and Macduff's children are sympathetically drawn: in

---

[17] Arcandam, sig. M 1 r.   [18] Dariot, sig. D 4 r.
[19] Hill, "Phisiognomie," appended to *Contemplation of Mankind.*
[20] Hill, leaf 110 [210].   [21] Arcandam, sig. M 3 r *et seq.*
[22] See the present writer, "Falstaff's Robin and Other Pages," *SP*, XXXVI, 476
et seq.

fact, one of the latter has a touch of manly choler. For these, the phlegmatic humor was not innate but the mere result of age, and so not a permanent disability or a matter for scorn.

According to Dariot, "a roūd face" and "faire eyes"[23] betokened the phlegmatic type under Venus; and, if Lady Macbeth's sex and "fair" complexion denote her truly, and if her "little hand" was proportionate to her body, then (whatever circumstances made her) her innate temper was also like Maria's, phlegmatic and shrewd and scheming to acquire the good things of this life. The "roūd" face" and "brown" color mentioned by Dariot as phlegmatic characteristics appear in the description of Octavia that the Messenger gives to Cleopatra:

> *Cle*. Bear'st thou her face in mind? is't long or round?
> *Mess*. Round, euen to faultinesse.
> *Cleo*. For the most part too, they are foolish that are so. Her haire what colour?
> *Mess*. Browne Madam: and her forehead
> As low as she could wish it.
> *Cleo*. There's Gold for thee. . . .

The phlegmatic type as reflected in Shakespeare from the physiology of the time s ems to fall into three groups: the first is fat, luxurious, and not too brave, like Sir Toby and Sir John; the second comprises chiefly children and women like Maria, small in stature, shrewd in mind, attractive in personality; and, if such persons preferred peace to war and luxury to hardship, it was but natural. The third type is lanky, cowardly, and stupid, with either a very thin or a very round face, soft hair that lies down readily and is of a pale color—like the gull Sir Andrew and like the silly Slender in *Merry Wives*. The first two of these types seem to fit the first of Dariot's astrological divisions, that under the "luxurious" and "effeminat" influence of the planet Venus; the last fits rather under the influence of the moon, which made men "faynt-hearted . . . fooles." This phlegm under Venus sometimes confuses with the sanguine

[23] Dariot, sig D 4 r.

humor; but phlegmatic men were hardly handsome, and were inclined to be cowardly and slothful.

In discussing phlegmatic psychology and character, most of the authorities seem chiefly to have in mind the more extreme type under the influence of the moon. According to Elyot, the man of phlegm is slow, dull in learning, and cowardly;[24] Batman declares him poor in health, "heauy and slow," dull, forgetful, soft of flesh, and fearful;[25] Lemnius says that the type is prone "to slouth, drowsynesse, bitternesse, sluggardy . . . rechlesse unheedynes," like Cloten in *Cymbeline,* that they are "nothing quicke," have a dull wit and base courage, that they are "lazye, slouthful, drowsie," hate exercise, like Falstaff, and crave "bellycheere."[26] Barrough seems to impute to them lethargy, gaping, and love of sleep;[27] and Niccholes advises a merchant or mariner to marry a phlegmatic wife "who can endure thy absence for weeks or months and still remain chaste."[28] This conception of the type in general accords with Dariot's lunar phlegm: "unstable . . . fearefull, faynt-hearted, prodigall . . . fooles, delighting in iourneis and variety of life."[29] He also, to be sure, says "thoughtful"; but the thoughts of "fooles" can hardly be intelligent. The phlegmatic person under Venus, he describes as "Gentle . . . affable . . . pittifull, . . . louing all ornaments . . . luxurious, giuen to idlenes and pleasures," and he also links this type with "ornaments and precious things and lusts."[30]

The phlegmatic type, soft and sluggish of body, timid of spirit, and often dull of mind, appears at best in Romeo's friend the well-wishing Benvolio, the confidant of his hopeless love for Rosaline and the would-be peacemaker between the feuding factions. His kindly efforts are somewhat ineffectual, and he fades from the play as the catastrophe draws on. Even as early as *Love's Labour's,* Shakespeare had used the humor for Constable Dull, whose "monster Ignorance" sired Dogberry's, and for the curate Sir Nathaniel, "a foolish

[24] Elyot, leaf 2 v.   [25] Batman, leaf 32 r.
[26] Lemnius, leaves 23 v, 81 r, 111 v.   [27] Barrough, pp. 24 *et seq.*
[28] A. Niccholes, *Discourse of Marriage* (London, 1615), p. 16.
[29] Dariot, sig. E 1.   [30] Dariot, sig. D 4 r.

man" and "soon dashed." It appears in his rustic clowns[31] and servants and especially in his great comic figures: in young Gobbo with his itch for fine livery and an easy life; in Falstaff's rag-tag following, especially Corporal Nym;[32] in the knight-by-purchase, Sir Andrew, and in the knights-by-braggadocio, Sir Toby Belch and Sir John Falstaff; in Slender, who cringes before Pistol's roaring; in Shallow, who toadies to Falstaff and is gulled for his pains; in Dogberry and the other parts of the famous comedian Will Kemp; and, with Kemp's retirement from the stage about 1600,[33] a less ridiculous and higher phlegmatic type grows commoner: in the "Simple, plain Clarence" of *Richard III* and in "dull" Casca in *Julius Caesar* Shakespeare had already started to develop it; in *Twelfth Night,* he shows some sympathy with Sir Toby's difficulties,[34] and gives him a happy ending; and, some years later, in Antony the phlegmatic type reaches even to tragic heights. The ludicrous gull Sir Andrew is toned down in *Othello* to the no-less-foolish but soberer Roderigo. In *Measure for Measure,* the well-intentioned but dilatory Duke seems to set forth the dangers of phlegm in the body politic, as Macbeth, at about this time, shows the dangers of the mercurial humor, Coriolanus of the choleric, and Lear of the melancholy. Phlegm was appropriate, not to rulers, but to women and children and such as lived for pleasure; and a phlegmatic Antony could come only to ruin. To be sure, it does not fit those independent-ladies whose presence in Elizabethan times Shakespeare reflects in Portia, the "merry wives," Beatrice, Olivia, Helena, and Emilia, and others; but it seems to belong to the more passive and idealized Queen of Richard II, to Blanch of Spain, to Hero in contrast with Beatrice, to Ophelia, to Desdemona after her marriage with Othello, to Mariana waiting and sorrowing at her "moated grange," to the frail Cressida, to the

[31] See the present writer, "Shakespeare's Rustic Servants," *Sh. Jhb.,* LXIX, 87 *et seq.*

[32] See the present writer, "The Humor of Corporal Nym," *Sh. Assoc. Bull.,* XII, 131 *et seq.*

[33] See T. W. Baldwin, *MLN,* XXXIX, 447.

[34] See the present writer, "Sir Toby's 'Cakes and Ale,'" *Eng. Studies,* XX, 57 *et seq.*

cast-off Catherine of Aragon and to those paragons of virtue, Isabella, Hermione, and Imogen. The humor appears perhaps most actively in Maria, who must exercise her wits in her quest for a husband. Most of these phlegmatic women, like Prince Arthur and Falstaff's Robin, are presented as passive sufferers from events that they cannot control: they are not in themselves dramatic, and do not make dramatic situations; but their suffering greatly heightens the pathos of catastrophe.

The professions and walks of life proper to phlegm under Venus are listed in Dariot as follows: "louers of delights . . . yong women, musitions, . . . lapidaries, embroiderers, and such like . . . it also signifieth mother, wife, damsels, concubins, yong men, cookes [e.g., the fat cook in *The Comedy of Errors*], kinswomen by blod, poets, paynters. . . ." Those under the less favorable influence of the moon are "messengers, shipmen, Queenes, Ladies, commanding, common people, fishers &c. al that labor in the waters . . . fooles, delighting in iourneis and variety of life . . . widow, mothers, & they which are in continuall motion, as legats, lackies &c." Some of these sorts of people either do not appear in Shakespeare or not enough to show any particular humor; but a number of the queens and ladies already noted and some of the young men clearly illustrate the passive, luxurious, and artistic temper that belongs with the phlegm of Venus: Brutus' lackey Lucius, that drowsy little singer, and the butler Stephano in *The Tempest,* seem to be examples; Ophelia and Desdemona sing; Viola declares that she will court the Duke's favor "in many sorts of music"; Rosencrantz in *Hamlet* loved the theater and was the king's legate to England; and the nature of Othello's wooing suggests that Desdemona took delight in "iourneis and variety of life."

Shakespeare's attitude toward the phlegmatic men of the earlier plays is generally satiric, and later grows more serious and even tragic. Of the satiric treatment, Dogberry, Sir Andrew, and Falstaff are the supreme examples; Shakespeare seems more sympathetic to Sir Toby; he idealizes the phlegmatic women of the tragedies and problem plays and late romances, and even Antoñy, shorn of his glories in the Delilah toils of Cleopatra, is made to arouse deep tragic pathos, if not quite respect. But Falstaff, Dogberry, and Sir Andrew would have inspired in the Elizabethans neither respect nor sympathy. Falstaff, indeed, added hypocrisy to debauchery, cowardice and bragging impudence, and so, to accord with his profession of swashbuckler-in-chief, assumed a choler though he had it not. But at his very entrance, his girth proclaims the deception and shows his inborn phlegmatic nature. He represents the more discreditable aspects of that humor: his lazy corpulence "lards the lean earth" when he cannot ride; at Gadshill, he flees before he even starts to fight, and tries to cover this poltroonery with boasting and big lies; in recruiting, he takes bribes; and he deliberately sends his soldiers to death so that he can draw their wages to line his own pockets; he revels in unpaid-for creature comforts at the tavern and at Mistress Quickly's house of sale; he stoops to poaching Shallow's deer, condones the picking of Slender's pocket, and tries with elephantine charms to seduce two worthy townswomen. The Elizabethans might forgive these latter peccadilloes set forth in *The Merry Wives of Windsor,* but certainly not the impudence, the hypocrisy, and, above all, the cowardice shown in the *Henry* plays.[35] If Falstaff is the craven debauchee of the phlegmatic humor, Constable Dogberry and Sir Andrew Aguecheek are its dolts par excellence, with a soft aroma of timidity apparent in Dogberry's instructions to the Watch and in Aguecheek's very name. Truly, Dogberry, a son of Constable Dull and a poor relation by bar sinister of Justice Shallow—Dogberry with his pompous parade of legal malapropisms, with his fine complacency of his fine figure and of the figure he cuts in town, with his maladroit airs and graces before the Governor and the Prince—this nonpareil of constables, for all future generations has been "writ down an Asse."[36] Such also is the inert Sir Andrew, whose speech is

[35] See Ruth E. Sims, "The Green Old Age of Falstaff," *Bull. Hist. Med.,* XIII, 144 *et seq.,* and the present writer, "Sir John Falstaff," *RES,* VIII, 414 *et seq.*

[36] See the present writer, "Dogberry's Due Process of Law," *JEGP,* XLII, 563 *et seq.*

pure vacuity, or mere parroting of others, who needs the constant promptings of Sir Toby to "accost" Maria and to conduct
his torpid wooing of Olivia, and even so is a laggard in love,
and whose timorous duel with Viola shows him also a dastard
in war. These three, Falstaff, Dogberry, and Sir Andrew, are
the apogee of Shakespeare's satirio-comic art; and all three are
compounds of phlegmatic traits of character.

Shakespeare's use of the phlegmatic type in serious situations is at first a bit wooden as in Hero or very incidental as
in Richard II's Queen; but, in Ophelia, he develops rather fully
a realistic pathos. She has the feminine charm and naïveté
and yielding passivity of the phlegmatic type: her only un-
prompted action is her artless love affair with the Crown
Prince in which unwittingly she plays with fire. At her
father's orders, she repulses him; and the shock of her father's
death unbalances her mind and so causes her suicide. In
short, she has the shy passivity of the ideal (not actual) Elizabethan woman—so much so that, to be convincing on the
stage, she has to be played as a very young girl of previously
secluded life.[37] In *Othello,* the Desdemona of Act I is entirely
Shakespeare's own, and like an independent Elizabethan girl
woos and weds her husband without benefit of parental advice
or even knowledge; but the married Desdemona of the later
acts that Shakespeare took from his Italian source, is as con-
ventual and naïve as Italian girls of the day:[38] she does not
believe that any woman could be faithless; even when Emilia
tells her, she cannot think that her husband could be jealous,
and continues stupidly to insist on Cassio's reinstatement;
and, even when her lord's malady is past all doubt, she can
do nothing but reassert her virtue. Like Hermione and Imogen, she is the luckless pawn of a Fate for which she is hardly
to be blamed; and perhaps this innocence justifies the somewhat forced happy endings of *The Winter's Tale* and *Cymbeline.* In these heroines, the phlegmatic type assumes, if not

[37] See the present writer, *The "Hamlet" of Shakespeare's Audience* (Durham,
N. C., 1938), chap. iv.

[38] See the present writer, "Desdemona," *Rev. Litt. Comp.,* XIII, 337 *et seq.*

a true *ethos,* at least deep tragic *pathos,* and thus heightens the emotion of the drama.

Mark Antony's character seems to have fascinated Shakespeare: Antony appears in two major plays, and is mentioned also in *Henry V* as "valiant" and in *Macbeth* as outshone by Octavius Caesar: slowly through the years, Shakespeare seems finally to have brought his personality into a unified focus. He appears in varying lights in three of Plutarch's *Lives;* and Plutarch, being interested as a biographer chiefly in fact, gives a somewhat disjointed characterization that implies at least three separate and rather conflicting humors. As Julius Caesar's chiefest courtier and colleague in the consulate and faithful friend, Antony seems sanguine; as a soldier and the boon companion of soldiers, a "valiant man" with "a minde bent to great enterprises," he seems choleric under the influence of Mars; as a deep-dyed sensualist, shown especially in his own biography, he seems phlegmatic under Venus. So indeterminate a character would hardly do for the main figure in a tragedy; and slowly this diversity in Shakespeare's mind gives way to unity.

In *Henry V,* it is the "valiant" Antony. In *Julius Caesar,* written about the same time, he appears in three complementary facets: as soldier, as playboy, and, most of all, as a sharp and sly politician. As noted in Plutarch, he curries popularity with the mob by pretending to be the "plaine, blunt," soldierly sort of man; and he fools Brutus into calling him "Wise" and "Valiant"; but he reveals his true opinion of the military when he sneers at Lepidus, "the tried and valiant soldier," as "a slight unmeritable man, Meet to be sent on errands." As a general, his ability is doubtful; for the Battle of Philippi is won, not so much by his strategy as by Brutus' errors. All this suggests that the "valiant" Antony of *Henry V* has given place to one whose martial choler is more assumed than real. The "*Antony* that Reuels long a-nights," that, like Rosencrantz, enjoys the theater and is "Gamesom," the "well beloued of Caesar," who is, therefore, apparently "fat"—this Antony who takes the goods the gods provide him, is evidently phlegmatic. After's Caesar's death appears a third Antony, the persuasive orator and scheming politician, the Antony that Cassius all along had feared. He saves himself by flattering the con- spirators and then the mob, thereupon turning against the former and cheating the latter of their just due in Caesar's will. This Antony should properly be of a cold, dry, crafty humor, mercurial, or, more likely, melancholy. Thus, though Shakespeare has obscured the sanguine traits of Plutarch, and made Antony's martial choler a mere disguise, yet the char- acter still is hardly unified. He is lightly sketched in the background of the play; a close examination shows little heroic about him; and one is left uncertain at the end whether his cold and calculating complexion is phlegmatic or mercurial or melancholy.

The reference in *Macbeth* suggests that in later years Shake- speare read Plutarch's "Antonius" rather than the "Brutus" or the "Caesar"; and the "Antonius," which Shakespeare closely follows in *Antony and Cleopatra,* especially develops the sen- sual aspect of its hero's character. The old story demanded a phlegmatic voluptuary, heedless of martial glory and of honor; and so Shakespeare depicts him. His victories are won by his generals, not himself. His followers refer to his soldierly spirit as a thing of the past; and, finally in disgust, even Enobarbus leaves him. Except for the marriage of convenience with Octavia, he shows little of the politician—certainly noth- ing of it in his dealings with Cleopatra; and all that remains is the confirmed voluptuary that cannot break his bonds. Cleopatra flatters him as "the greatest soldier in the world"; but that is merely part of her amorous technique. The very first speech in the play strikes the keynote, and declares that he is no longer a soldier but has become a debauchee "To coole a Gypsies Lust." Antony enters, and tells Cleopatra that he has not art to reckon his love for her; at news from Rome, he is impatient; and, though he knows that he must break "these strong Egyptian Fetters" or lose himself in "dotage," yet he is so confirmed in his "idlenesse" with "this enchanting Queene" that he becomes womanish and neglects both political and military affairs. Young Pompey calls him "This amorous Surfetter," the "nere Lust-wearied *Antony*," and looks forward hopefully to the effects on Antony's mind and body:

> . . . all the charmes of Love,
> Salt *Cleopatra,* soften thy wand lip,
> Let Witchcraft join with Beauty, Lust with both,
> Tye up the Libertine in a field of Feasts,
> Keepe his Braine fuming; Epicurean Cookes,
> Sharpen with cloylesse sauce his Appetite;
> That sleepe and feeding may prorogue his Honour
> Even till Lethied dulnesse—

And Antony himself in the feast with Lepidus and Octavius looks forward to the moment when "the conquering Wine hath steept our sense In soft and delicate Lethe." This is the language of a sybarite; and well may his soldiers declare that they are "Women's men." When he followed Cleopatra's barge in flight from Actium, truly he "kist away Kingdomes and Provinces"; and Scarrus well remarks:

> I neuer saw an Action of such shame;
> Experience, Man-hood, Honor, ne're before
> Did violate so itselfe.

Indeed, he knows that he has come to "shame" and "dishonor"; and yet a "kisse" repays him for it all. When Octavius lands triumphant at Alexandria, Antony cries out for "one other gawdy night." To be sure, he offers to meet his enemy in single combat; but this bravado is refused. At last, Antony declares, "This fowle Egyptian hath betrayed me" and calls her "triple-turn'd Whore"; but, even as he is dying, he seeks her yet again. This is indeed the last infirmity of a noble mind, the phlegmatic influence of Venus borne up to tragic heights by Shakespeare's sympathetic artistry.

Sanguine is the glorious humor of Shakespeare's heroes and lovers. The phlegmatic, starting basely as the humor for his ludicrous dolts and cowards, became the humor for his chil-

dren and more passive heroines, and at last even for the
supreme lover of all his plays. Marlowe's Edward II sank himself in debauchery and grudgingly paid the price; but Antony
threw an empire away and flung along with it all manliness
and honor, knew Cleopatra false and yet must love her, and
cried out, even as his life blood flowed away:

> I am dying, Egypt, dying; onely
> I heere importune death a-while, vntill
> Of many thousand kisses, the poore last
> I lay vpon thy lippes.

CHAPTER IV

THE CHOLERIC TYPE

The choleric (bilious) humor was hot and dry in direct contrast to the cold and moist phlegmatic; it gave strength to the body and the mind, and so was proud and independent. That rough-and-tumble age required such a humor; and Shakespeare's plays mention *choler* and *choleric* some forty times, and provide characters, like Nym and. Falstaff, who assume this temper for convenience, and also more than thirty bona fide examples: some of these are blunt, honest soldiers, men of a word and a blow, like Tybalt, Capulet, Hotspur, Glendower, Fluellen, Fortinbras, Othello, Cassio, Macduff, Enobarbus, and Coriolanus; some are rulers or courtiers like Longaville and Biron in *Love's Labour's,* or Valentine in *Two Gentlemen,* who "hunts" for "honor," or the Bastard of Faulconbridge, Henry V, Claudio in *Much Ado,* Laertes, Bertram, Brabantio, and the jealous Leontes; some, born to low degree, fall through choleric pride and inordinate ambition into the ludicrous, like Bottom the weaver, Dr. Caius, Master Ford, and the pushing Malvolio; and some through pride fall to tragic depths, like Cassius, King Claudius, Iago, and Coriolanus; some are the new independent women of the age, who woo husbands for themselves and may even deceive or disobey their parents, such as Kate, Juliet, Rosalind, Olivia, Cordelia, Miranda, and in more dreadful guise, Goneril and Regan. These choleric characters are active and dynamic; they make events and keep the plot in motion. They are the very stuff of drama and especially of tragedy with its catastrophic clash of wills.

Different writers subdivide the choleric type in various

ways; but, astrologically, it falls into two groups, those more violent under the planet Mars, appropriate to soldiers and ambitious schemers, and those more pleasing under the benign influence of the sun, including courtiers like Biron and Valentine and heroines like Juliet and Olivia. The former group, according to Dariot, is "fierie . . . the lesse misfortune, mas-[culine,] of the night, intemperat." It has a tendency to hatred and envy, and "hath redd haire, woundes chiefly in the face." Physiologically, it is related to the "Left eare, gall, raynes, vaynes and their diseases," to "fevers, plagues, jaundice, ulsers, madness, swellings, gout, maladies of the skin, woundes, and death by iron or fire." Its color is red; its metal, iron; its alchemical element, fire; and it is "bitter like gall, sharp, yellow, fiery";[1] and, quite appropriately "this yellow Iachimo" in *Cymbeline* seems to show all the worst traits of choler. Heat, fire, and dryness, Shakespeare again and again associates with this humor and with the martial ardor of his votaries: the unbridled Hotspur, who is "altogether governed by humours" and by his "spleen," and is "drunk with choler," has "heat of blood," and is "dry with rage" of battle. Indeed, the plays repeatedly use *fiery* in the metaphoric senses of *spirited* or *irritable*.

Choler under the influence of the sun, according to Dariot, is temperate and more fortunate: to this category belong the charming Juliet, whom the text repeatedly associates with the sun, and Henry V, England's hero-monarch, whose eye gives "A largess universal like the sun," and whose "good heart" is itself "the sun . . . for it shines bright and never changes." Indeed, the Constable of France marvels that from a land where there is so little sunlight as in England the soldiers should be so brave. Dariot describes the sun's man as "diurnall, fayre croceal, crisp [of] hayr, bald, of a fayre colour." This complexion especially belongs to "the sight, sinews, hart and right side," and is subject to cramps, swooning, fluxes, and maladies of the mouth, stomach, and liver. It is of good odor, golden, ruddy, white, and purple.[2] The type was appropriate

[1] Dariot, sig. D 3 r.   [2] *Ibid.*, D 3 v.

to fine gentlemen and *grandes dames,* and approached the sanguine humor; but Lemnius differentiates choler as hastier in
speech, more scornful, bitter, and scurrilous:[3] he seems to have
had in mind mainly the former, martial sort, which was more
pronounced and so more readily distinguished. As Schmidt's
Lexicon attests, Shakespeare repeatedly uses the heart to express courage and other strong emotions; and courtiers and
soldiers should be "fayre" and have well-developed sinews.
As in the case of Hotspur already noted, Shakespeare often
associates choler with the spleen, an organ more usually considered melancholy; but Lemnius considers it closely linked
with the stomach,[4] which Dariot does list, and in which, according to Elyot, choler was "decoct or boyled."[5]   In the
quarrel-scene, Brutus will not have Cassius vent on him the
venom of his "spleen"; and again and again, Shakespeare
relates the spleen to heat and violence, as in "youthful spleen
and warlike rage," in the "heated spleen" of soldiers, in
"spleen and fury," and in "arrogancy, spleen and pride." He
repeatedly refers to the liver as the seat of courage, as when
Fabian urges Sir Andrew to "put fire in your heart, and brim-
stone in your liver." He commonly uses *gall* referring at once
to the secretion and to the bitterness of mind it caused, as
when Emilia tells Desdemona that wives "have galls" and
therefore, if abused, will take "revenge." In Moth's "dangerous rhyme" in the second scene of *Love's Labour's,* white and
red seem to refer not only to colors of the lady's face, but also
to her astral complexion:

> If she be made of white and red,
>   Her faults will ne'er be known;
> For blushing cheeks by faults are bred,
>   And fears by pale white shown:
>
> Then if she fear, or be to blame,
>   By this you shall not know;
> For still her cheeks possess the same
>   Which native she doth owe.

[3] Lemnius, leaf 99 v.   [4] *Ibid.,* leaf 138 v *passim.*   [5] Elyot, leaf 9.

In short, he seems to be suggesting that red and white, being choleric colors, may conceal evil or violence. But the poetic allusions in the plays to the humors and complexions are without number; and the present study is concerned rather with humoral use in plot or character.

The dry heat of choler[6] was thought to affect the heart and so the whole physique.[7] Thus choleric anger enflames the entire body "with a sodaine burning heate,"[8] a "boyling,"[9] more precisely described as a "boyling of the Bloud aboute the Heart, wherewith the Braine also being excited by choler, is set in a heate and testines, desyrous of reveng, whensoever any iniury is offered."[10]   *Henry VI,* Part I, refers to "boiling choler"; in *Midsummer-Night's Dream,* Pyramus "bravely" broaches to the lion his "boiling bloody breast"; and, in *Lear,* the "heat of Gloucester's displeasure . . . rageth in him." The humor had also its good and necessary bodily functions; as Vaughan explains: "Cholericke humour is hot and fiery, bitter, and like unto the flowre of wine. It serveth not onely to cleanse the guts of filth, but also to make the liver hot, to hinder the bloud from putrefaction."[11] Vicary,[12] Walkington,[13] and Churchyard[14] declare such persons "lean." Elyot attributes to them a "Voyce sharpe"[15] like that of Coriolanus; and Hill, a forehead "vallied, depressed and hollow";[16] but Ptolemy supposes the sons of Mars "sturdy" and handsome.[17] This spareness of choler is well exemplified in Cassius, whose "lean and hungry look" aroused the misgivings of Caesar;[18] and Falstaff (with his tongue in his cheek) justified his pressing of such diseased and undernourished scarecrows for the army in place of the more substantial Bullcalf (who could bribe his way out), on the basis of choleric "spirit":

[6] Walkington, p. 76.
[7] Elyot, leaf 62 v.
[8] Bullein, leaf 24 v.
[9] Coeffeteau, p. 552.
[10] Lemnius, leaf 128.
[11] Vaughan, p. 28.
[12] Vicary, p. 47.
[13] Walkington, p. 109.
[14] T. Churchyard, *Mirror of Man* (London, 1594).
[15] Elyot, leaf 2 v.
[16] Hill, leaf 28 v.
[17] Ptolemy, p. 149.
[18] See the present writer, "Cassius and Brutus," *Bull. Hist. Med.,* XIII, 133 *et seq.*

Care I for the limb, the thewes, the stature, bulk, and big assemblance of a man! Give me the spirit, Master Shallow. . . . And this same half-faced fellow, Shadow; give me this man: he presents no mark to the enemy; the foeman may with as great aim level at the edge of a penknife. And for a retreat; how swiftly will this Feeble the woman's tailor run off! O, give me the spare men, and spare me the great ones.[19]

Napoleon is credited with seriously holding some such sentiments. Many of these choleric characters, furthermore, especially the courtiers and great ladies, should undoubtedly be handsome. In short, Shakespeare quite properly associates with choler, fire and heat and the liver, spleen and gall.

Elyot links choler with summer, from the ides of May until the ides of August and with the third to the ninth hour of the day, and remarks that the humor was most powerful in warm weather.[20] Vaughan also puts the choleric hours between the third and the ninth in the morning[21] when warmth is increasing; and Lemnius associates choler with summer's heat.[22] Very likely for this reason, Shakespeare shifted the action of *Romeo and Juliet* from winter and early spring where he found it in his sources, to the middle of July, with its "mad blood stirring."[23] At the very beginning of the tragedy, the play on the word *choler* strikes the keynote; and Juliet declares that her "bud of love" was matured by "summer's ripening breath." The choleric hours seem to be illustrated in the career of "fiery" and "furious" Tybalt, who admits his "wilful choler": Old Capulet can entreat him to a peace in the phlegmatic evening; and, on Monday afternoon, a phlegmatic day and melancholy hour, when his choleric nature would be at its weakest, Romeo kills him. The cure of Kate's choler in *The Taming of the Shrew* seems to take place appropriately in the chill and damp of winter; and Dr.

---

[19] See the present writer, "Sir John Falstaff," *RES*, VIII, 414 *et seq.;* and *II Henry IV*, III, ii, 251 *et seq.*

[20] Elyot, leaves 70-72.

[21] Vaughan, p. 126.

[22] Lemnius, leaves 86, 99, 127.

[23] See the present writer, "Shakespeare's 'Star-Crossed Lovers,'" *RES*, XV, 16 *et seq.*

Caius associates hot weather with his *"grande affaire"* of the heart.

Choler was naturally associated with youth and early middle age: Laurentius places it between twenty-four and forty;[24] Cuffe between twenty-five and fifty;[25] and Cogan in the period of youth. This would be the martial time of life; and most of Shakespeare's choleric figures are soldiers, or at least head-strong and self-willed. This is the proper humor for Hotspur, whose very nickname shows his character, for Tybalt, "a gentleman of the very first house" (a punning reference perhaps to Aries, the first, and choleric, sign of the zodiac), for the "proper" Cassio, for the peppery Dr. Caius,[26] and for such wilful heroines as Kate, Juliet, and Cordelia. By the same token, the first scene of *Lear* should be in summertime, when the blood even of the aged King was hot and not to be gainsaid.

A choleric condition in an individual might arise from the position of the planets and constellations at his birth or from his age or from the season of the year; but the Elizabethans seem to have thought of it as arising more particularly from some immediate cause, physical or psychological. Thus strong drink or highly seasoned or burnt foods put choler in the blood and this in turn caused anger.[27] If one had an innate tendency toward the humor, drunkenness, by removing social inhibitions, revealed one's natural self,[28] and, if one were choleric one got drunk more quickly and also was more likely to be "intemperat";[29] for drinking gave "unnatural heat,"[30] and this in turn increased both thirst and choler, and so set up a vicious circle. Intoxication from ale lasted longer than from wine;[31] and red wine was more heating, and so more dangerous, than white.[32] The dryness of choler also caused "inordinate thirst."[33] Thus choler caused drunkenness, and drunkenness

[24] Laurentius, p. 174.   [25] Cuffe, p. 118.
[26] See J. L. Stender, "Master Doctor Caius," *Bull. Hist. Med.*, VIII, 113 *et seq*.
[27] Walkington, p. 103.
[28] Vaughan, pp. 26 *et seq*.; Wright, p. 208.
[29] Dariot, sig. D 3 r.   [30] Bullein, leaf 22; *Regimen*, leaf 31 r.
[31] *Ibid.*, leaf 55 r.   [32] Cogan, p. 206.
[33] Batman, leaf 25 r.

increased choler. Moreover, wine helped choler by beclouding the reason:[34] thus the body of "A Drunkard . . . becomes at last a miry way, where the spirits are beclogged and cannot pass. . . . All the use he has of this vessel himself, is to hold thus much."[35] Lemnius differentiates the varying effects of wine on different people and at different stages of intoxication: the first type, on becoming "cupshot" is "contentious and brawling"; some are "stil" and moody; some "verye blabbatiue"; some "weeping, howling."[36] Wright says, "some are mery mad, some melancholy mad, some furious, others fainting. . . ."[37] On the other hand, wine was a recognized palliative for a naturally phlegmatic temper or for the melancholy cold of old age;[38] but, even in this, it was dangerous because it dissolved vital moisture.[39] Falstaff uses it amply as a specific against his natural phlegm and the melancholy of age;[40] sack makes even Trinculo bold; but in *Lear,* the heat of the old King's choler, even without wine, burns out his vital fluids.[41]

Heavy drinking was a characteristic Elizabethan vice, inveighed against especially by military writers like Sutcliffe, Riche, and Digges,[42] for it ruined army discipline and bred disastrous quarrels. Shakespeare repeatedly depicts drunkenness: in the more phlegmatic Falstaff, in Sir Toby, and in Stephano in *The Tempest,* it serves merely to tone the spirit up to manly ardor; and Lady Macbeth likewise uses it to make herself "bold" enough to play her part in the regicide; but, in a figure like Cassio, whose courtliness suggests the choler of the sun, and whose profession implies the choler of Mars, the effect of wine should be—and is—both rapid and devastating. Iago has arranged a drinking party including two Cypriote gallants, Cassio and himself; and, in politeness, Cassio cannot refuse. He demurs, but the demands of Iago

---

[34] Coeffeteau, p. 612.

[35] J. Earle, *Microcosmographie,* "A Drunkard."

[36] Lemnius, leaf 149 r.   [37] Wright, p. 207.

[38] Cogan, p. 193.   [39] Lemnius, leaf 118 r.

[40] See Ruth E. Sims, "The Green Old Age of Falstaff," *Bull. Hist. Med.,* XIII, 144 *et seq.*

[41] "The Old Age of King Lear," *JEGP,* XXXIX, 527 *et seq.*

[42] See the present writer, "Captain General Othello," *Ang.,* XLIII, 307-308.

and of courtesy overcome his scruples. By drink, he soon degenerates to "wrath" and so from a "sensible man" to a "fool" and then a "beast." At first he is "mery mad," and praises Iago's song; then he suddenly turns moody and religious, and once or twice remembers his place as head of the guard. This seems to remind him of his superior rank as lieutenant, and he shows his inner choleric pride, and declares that as a commissioned officer and a gentleman, he must have precedence even in salvation—a remark that would cut Iago to the quick. Iago, however, is smooth as butter, and as slippery. Cassio declares he is not drunk, and undertakes to prove it by telling his right hand from his left. He goes out to set the watch, there meets and fights with the silly Roderigo, and so the "mutiny" that Iago wished has been achieved. No wonder that Iago describes Cassio as "choleric"; for the latter goes through the very stages of intoxication described in writers on choler.[43] In other respects as well, he shows himself choleric: he is elegant and courtly with Desdemona; his virility requires the ministrations of the compliant Bianca; his keen sense of honor is so crushed by his drunken lapse that he cannot bring himself directly to ask for reinstatement, but, at Iago's suggestion, attempts it through the mediation of Desdemona, and so gives color to Othello's jealousy. By nature, he is, like Juliet, the choleric type under the influence of the sun, courtly and charming; but strong drink aggravates this choler so that his pride and irritability become unbearable, and misfortune shortly follows.

Not only alcohol but also "much eating," peppery condiments, mustard and burnt food,[44] dangerously increased choler, as Walkington quotes from Galen. "Dry" food as a choleric stimulant is mentioned in the dialogue between the two Syracusians in the second act of *The Comedy of Errors;* and, in *The Taming of the Shrew*,[45] this matter of choleric diet forms

[43] See the present writer, "The Choleric Cassio," *Bull. Hist. Med.*, VII, 383 *et seq.*

[44] Walkington, pp. 103-104.

[45] See the present writer, " 'Kate the Curst,' " *Jour. Nerv. Ment. Dis.*, LXXXIX, 757 *et seq.*

a major episode in the plot. Petruchio has determined to cure the high-spirited and violent Kate of her dangerous choler and subdue her to wifely obedience. During the courtship, he submissively endures all the tantrums of this "fiend of hell"; but, at the wedding, the cure begins. He is taking a great risk; for he himself appears to have a tendency toward her humor; and, as Ferrand remarks, the marriage of two choleric persons "is rather slavery then true Loue, it is so subject to Outrages and Anger."[46] Shakespeare later treats this same problem in Benedick and Beatrice,[47] and in Bertram and Helena. Petruchio's therapeutic method is to out-Herod Herod: he comes to the wedding crazily arrayed, rants and rails during the ceremony, and will not stay for the feast. At every point, he crosses his wife's desires, and "kills her in her own humor." Perhaps with special reason, he follows the old custom of drinking sweet muscadel after the ceremony, for muscadel was thought to augment choler.[48] On the road home, Kate's hot, dry humor is subjected to rain and mud and cold so that she arrives "almost frozen to death" in a house where not even the fire is lit. At dinner, she is denied mustard as "too hot" for her; and Petruchio orders the food, which he declares is "burnt," to be taken from the table:

> 'Tis burnt; and so is all the meat.
> What dogs are these! Where is the rascal cook?
> How durst you, villains, bring it from the dresser . . .
> I tell thee, Kate, 'twas burnt and dried away,
> And I expressly am forbid to touch it,
> For it engenders choler, planteth anger;
> And better 'twere that both of us did fast,
> Since, of ourselves, ourselves are choleric,
> Than feed it with such over-roasted flesh.

This treatment of "cold cheer," he continues with continence on the marriage-night, and starvation, so that finally Kate becomes a model wife, and in the last act shows herself obedient

---

[46] Ferrand, p. 93. See also Coeffeteau, p. 623; and A. Niccholes, *Discourse of Marriage* (London, 1615), p. 14.

[47] See the present writer, "Benedick and Beatrice," *JEGP*, XLI, 140 *et seq.*

[48] Walkington, p. 104, and Coeffeteau, p. 612.

to his beck and call. Petruchio is a successful practitioner, for her cure seems to be complete and lasting.

Not only physical but also psychological causes could augment this humor to the danger point. Misfortunes could cause choler,[49] such as Jessica's elopement and theft of Shylock's jewels.[50] Envy "arising from other mens felicity,"[51] from the disdain of friends,[52] or of inferiors[53] might furnish a more or less lasting cause; Downame gives the sources of anger as self-love, "pride and arrogancie";[54] and contempt of others[55] and belief of talebearers[56] also might play a part. Indeed, almost all of these imbued Iago with vitriolic bitterness:[57] his old friend and commander had passed him over for promotion in favor of a courtly fellow of less experience, and so wounded his pride and cut off his ambition to become a commissioned officer and so a "gentleman"; Iago, moreover, had heard whispers against Othello and his wife. He was a soldier, and so by profession choleric and of necessity chary of his honor; and such imputations struck at the manhood that was his very stock-in-trade. In that age of growing feminine independence—well exemplified in Emilia's talk—jealousy was a danger to which husbands filled with choleric pride were particularly prone; and Shakespeare uses it as a comic motive in *Merry Wives*, tragic in *Lear* and *Othello*, and romantic in the *A Midsummer-Night's Dream* and *The Winter's Tale*. In *Othello*, it appears most violently in the title role; but Iago illustrates it in more of its aspects, indeed in three of the four types set forth in Varchi's tract. Bullein notes that some men are naturally jealous,[58] and La Primaudaye and Varchi[59] attribute this characteristic to the choleric humor. Ferrand associates it with hot southern countries;[60] and some thought

[49] Coeffeteau, p. 580.
[50] See the present writer, "The Psychology of Shylock," *Bull. Hist. Med.*, VIII. 643 *et seq.*
[51] Vaughan, p. 141.   [52] Coeffeteau, pp. 587, 590.
[53] *Ibid.*, p. 589.   [54] Downame, leaves 25, 26, 59, 60.
[55] Coeffeteau, pp. 559 *passim.*   [56] Downame, leaf 30.
[57] Varchi, *passim.* See also the present writer, "The Jealousy of Iago," *Neophil.*, XXV, 50 *et seq.*   [58] Bullein, leaf 26 r.
[59] La Primaudaye, p. 312; Varchi, pp. 24, 29.
[60] Ferrand, pp. 89-93.

it a necessary adjunct to true love.[61]   Iago as a soldier is choleric, and, as a Venetian, has the hot blood of the south. Just as drunkenness and choler set up a vicious circle, so jealousy also both caused[62] and was caused by it.[63]   Brathwait,[64] Coeffeteau,[65] Varchi,[66] Ferrand,[67] Bullein,[68] and others, all agree on its tormenting frenzies.   Iago calls it "a Greene-ey'd Monster"; and Varchi terms it a "frightful Monster, and infernall Fury" and an "insatiable Monster."[69] Iago calls it a "poysonous Minerall"; and Varchi terms it a "black poyson,"[70] and declares that it leads to "reuengements, & the most horrible and sauage murthers,"[71] as indeed it did in Shakespeare's tragedy. Iago, moreover, in his jealousy follows the choleric pattern set forth in Plutarch and illustrated later and more fully in Shakespeare's Coriolanus:[72] outraged pride leading to moody anger and this to revenge and so to catastrophe.   The circumstances and Iago's comparatively humble status required of him a greater secrecy and so a hypocritical good nature; but his fundamental humor is the same as that of Coriolanus, who betrayed his countrymen because they were ungrateful for his having saved them.

Thus many causes besides the planet ascendant at one's birth might superinduce choler or augment to the danger point a choleric humor already dominant: the time of life or of the year, a heating or dry diet, envy of others or disdain by them, ambitious pride and professional or sexual jealousy. These were causes and also symptoms of the choleric humor, and so appear more or less in Othello, in Cassio, and in the secret motives of Iago.   Huarte sums up his conception of the choleric character: "The ordinaree conditions of men hot and dry in the third degree, are courage, pride, liberalitie, audacitie,

[61] Coeffeteau, pp. 175 *et seq.;* Varchi, pp. 55-56.
[62] La Primaudaye, pp. 312-314; Downame, leaf 32; Coeffeteau, pp. 580, 627-628.
[63] Varchi, pp. 24, 29.
[64] R. Brathwait, *English Gentlewoman* (London, 1631), p. 36.
[65] Coeffeteau, p. 180.   [66] Varchi, p. 5.
[67] Ferrand, p. 91.   [68] Bullein, leaf 26 r.
[69] Varchi, pp. 9, 51.   [70] *Ibid.,* p. 9.
[71] *Ibid.,* p. 59.
[72] See the present writer, "Shakespeare's Coriolanus," *West Va. U. Phil. Bull.,* 1939, pp. 22 *et seq.*

and cheerfulnesse, and a good grace and pleasantnesse, and in matter of women such a one hath no bridle nor ho."[73]   This description suggests the sanguine type which resembled choler under the sun's influence; but most writers rather have in mind the more violent martial choler. The sufferer from this humor was "full of grief and bitternesse";[74] and Bright discusses his psychology at some length:

A man of hastie disposition, readie to answere, and quicke witted, will make reply to that which should be said, before the tale be half told, whereby he faileth in his replication, and answereth from the purpose: . . . This appeareth plaine in Cholericke persons, or such as are disposed to anger: such are offended where they have no cause in truth but by mistaking [like Othello and Iago]: and where they have cause, the vehemency of the apprehension, and the braine unto the seat of perturbation, inforceth double passion: especially when the heart is as flexible, as the braine is light, then rangeth it unto all extremitie.[75]

Lemnius associates the humor with "chyding . . . fighting, murther, robbery, sedition."[76] Coeffeteau attributes to it the greatest "violence" of all the passions; indeed, none is "worse or more dangerous."[77]   Downame says that unjust anger "maketh men like the deuill."[78] All this arose from the initial choleric sin of pride and its consequences, ambition and revenge: Dariot calls choleric men "ambitious."[79]   La Primaudaye,[80] Adams,[81] and Coeffeteau[82] associate choler and ambition; and this might lead to a dangerous "discontentment"[83] and the slights that actuated revenge.[84] Such must have been the evolution of Iago's professional jealousy against Othello.

Choleric persons were thought to be quick-witted in speech and action, like Beatrice and Benedick in *Much Ado:* Elyot attributes to them a "Witte sharpe and quicke";[85] "Dr. Arcan-

[73] Huarte, p. 280.
[74] Coeffeteau, p. 559.
[75] Bright, p. 115.
[76] Lemnius, leaf 23 v.
[77] Coeffeteau, p. 598.
[78] Downame, leaf 48 r.
[79] Dariot, sig. D 3 v.
[80] La Primaudaye, pp. 313-314.
[81] Adams, pp. 39-40.
[82] Coeffeteau, p. 567.
[83] Wright, p. 308.
[84] Vaughan, p. 136.
[85] Elyot, leaf 2 v.

dam" finds them "prompt of wit";[86] Huarte attributes this wit
to the heat and dryness of the humor;[87] and Wright associates
wit with choler.[88] Thus "Bully" Bottom, whose "chief humor is for a tyrant" and who longs to "roar" in the part of
the lion, has both "the best person" and "the best wit" of "any
handicraft man in Athens."

Hill describes the humor as "obstinate";[89] but the authority
of Galen made several writers call it "inconstant,"[90] "vn-
stable,"[91] and "changeable."[92] Iago certainly illustrates unswerv-
ing obstinacy in the pursuit of his revenge; inconstancy,
Shakespeare seems to associate rather with the mercurial temper as illustrated in the person of Macbeth; but apparently
Emilia was quite willing to be inconstant to Iago; the violent
choleric jealousy of Othello utterly changed his love for Desdemona; and Iago's choleric pride nullified his years of association with Othello.

The social groups most subject to martial choler according
to Dariot were as follows: "All warriers, brawlers, contumeli-
ous persons, coniurers, quarrellers, theeues, drunkards, . . .
physitions, Chirurgiens, turks, yreful, violent . . . leaders of
armies . . . gunmakers, cutlers, a melter of metals . . . al-
cumist. . . ."[93] Under solar choler belong kings, courtiers,
lovers, and others who suggest the sanguine humor.[94] Lemnius,[95] Riche,[96] and Huarte[97] associate choler with war. The
social effects of the humor in its more extreme state were disastrous. The ambition that attended it was regarded as "most
dangerous"[98] and "wicked."[99] As in the case of Othello and
Iago, this humor "overthroweth all friendship."[100] It was
"venomous,"[101] led to "brawling"[102] and dire revenge.[103] In-

[86] Arcandam, sig. M 2 r.   [87] Huarte, pp. 26, 57, 280.
[88] Wright, pp. 212-213.   [89] Hill, leaf 8 v.
[90] Arcandam, sig. M 2 r.   [91] Huarte, p. 5.
[92] Walkington, pp. 107-109.   [93] Dariot, sig. D 3 r.
[94] *Ibid.,* sig D 3 v.   [95] Lemnius, leaf 23.
[96] See *Twelfth Night,* ed. Furness var., p. 329.
[97] Huarte, p. 205.
[98] R. R[ogers], *The Anatomie of the Minde* (London, 1576), leaf 10.
[99] R. Cleaver, *Godly Form* (London, 1598), p. 68.
[100] Downame, leaf 56 r; Coeffeteau, p. 606.
[101] Batman, leaf 32 v.
[102] Downame, leaf 49; Dariot, sig. D 3 r.
[103] Downame, leaf 26; Coeffeteau, pp. 550, 555, 557, 615-616.

deed, it was the worst of all human tendencies, and was responsible for "all the miseries and ruins which happen in the world."[104]

Not only is *Othello* a play of conflicting choleric temperaments, but so also is *Coriolanus*.[105] The noble Roman (patterned closely after Plutarch) is introduced with repeated reference to his "insolence" and "pride"; he condemns the vulgar commons; and, when he asks for votes as consul, he will not even show his wounds as custom required and as he had done in Plutarch: thus Shakespeare went so far as to change his source to increase the pride of his hero. Mars is Coriolanus' particular deity; Coriolanus is the "Flower of warriors," indeed, "bred i' the wars Since he could draw a sword"; and he is "bolder" than the "devil." As a soldier, he is "avid of fame," and by a miracle of valor takes the city of the rival Corioli single-handed; and Shakespeare follows Plutarch in making him "so chollericke and impacient that he would yeeld to no living creature." He drinks "hot wine" unmixed with water; and his "grim looks" and terrible voice bespeak the choleric man. In vain does Menenius try to "cure" his "disease": Coriolanus himself declares that to be "milder" would be "False to my nature." His choleric temper runs afoul of the plebeians and their choleric tribunes; and choleric people did not get along with one another. Thus started the bitter feud that ruined Coriolanus and almost ruined Rome: he runs the gamut of pride, choler, revenge, and ultimate catastrophe. The Tribunes incite the commons to vote against him for the consulship; and thus he has to experience the disdain of inferiors that was an especial occasion for choleric bitterness. The leaders of the plebeians had hoped that this would "Put him in choler straight"; and, indeed, it so much does so that he turns against Rome, and thus illustrates the inconstancy of his humor. He leads a Volscian army to lay waste to his native land; Rome is in despair; all embassies fail to move him; but finally his mother persuades him to

[104] Coeffeteau, pp. 599, 617.
[105] See the present writer, "Coriolanus," *cit. supra.*

desist, and he makes peace. The Volscians denounce him as a "traitor." He is furious, and in his fury ruins his defense by reminding them of their many defeats at Roman hands. The Volscian "People" set on him, and he dies in outraged pride and choler. Thus the choleric hero could live neither with the choleric Romans nor with the choleric Volscians. Perhaps the Elizabethans would have blamed his ruin partly on the weakness and faction of democracy; and Coriolanus, if a Renaissance king, would have been an altogether admirable figure—though a thought too tactless and fiery. At all events, he is a great tragic protagonist, a heroic figure brought low by a single dram of evil in his nature.

Dariot divides choler astrologically into that under Mars, which in extreme form might end, like melancholy, in an insane fury, and Othello and Coriolanus come near this state; and that under the sun, more genial and restrained like the sanguine type and illustrated not only in sundry courtiers and great ladies but also in the hero-king of the Elizabethans, Henry V, the victor of Agincourt. He will not go to war without being assured by the highest ecclesiastical authorities that his cause is just; he considers the dangers from Scotland. When the French embassy arrives, he declares that he is a true "Christian king" and therefore can control his "passion" so that they need have no fear in stating their message plainly. Although their speech has elements of insult, he answers with good-humored dignity. "Now all the youth of England is on fire," and the war begins. The King shows at once his clemency and his firmness by forgiving a man who "rail'd against our person" but ordering the execution of the nobles who took French bribes to overthrow the government. Even his enemies describe him as "modest in exception" but "terrible in constant resolution." The "vanities" of his youth were merely "Covering discretion with a coat of folly," and this coat is now cast off. At the siege of Harfleur, he again combines "mercy" with fortitude, and the town capitulates. He orders that the inhabitants of the country through which the army goes be justly treated, and approves Bardolph's execution for theft. He personally mingles with the soldiery "With cheerful semblance" before Agincourt, so that "every wretch, pining and pale before ... plucks comfort from his looks." Even the inglorious Pistol gives him a panegyric as "a bawcock and a heart of gold ... of fist most valiant." When Agincourt is won, he gives his thanks to God. Peace is declared, and he woos the Princess of France—as far as "a plain king" can be a courtly wooer; and he plainly tells the lady: "take me, take a soldier; take a soldier, take a king." Thus, as the Epilogue declares, "most greatly lived, This star of England."

Most writers refer to choler only in its more extreme and dangerous aspects. Vaughan divides it into "open" and "hidden"[106]—the former like Cassio, the latter like Iago. Elyot allows for four types of choler:[107] that mixed with a large amount of blood would doubtless be Dariot's choler of the sun as in Henry V; in Shylock, it seems to be mixed with melancholy;[108] but one can hardly imagine what it would be like when mixed with its opposite phlegm. Walkington divides it into natural and not natural,[109] depending apparently on whether the choler was innate as in Hotspur and Glendower or acquired because of one's age, profession, or some circumstance of the moment. Coeffeteau, following Aristotle, differentiates three sorts of choler, respectively delineated in the characters of Cassio, Iago, and Othello: sudden, acute but quickly over, like a drunken brawl; long-continued, sharp, bitter, and secret, appropriate to plotters and deep schemers; "violent" and without rest until revenge is taken, like the fury of Othello.[110] In like fashion, Downame distinguishes several sorts of anger:[111] one soon started and soon over, one slow to start and slow to end, one rapid in its beginning but slow to stop. Indeed, the choleric humor was complex in its psychological reactions.

The ready wit of the choleric man under the sun's influence was one of his most attractive traits. It appears in the cour-

---

[106] Vaughan, p. 136. [107] Elyot, leaf 8 v.
[108] See the present writer, "The Psychology of Shylock," *Bull. Hist. Med.*, VIII, 643 *et seq.*
[109] Walkington, p. 107. [110] Coeffeteau, pp. 571 *et seq.*
[111] Downame, leaf 39 v. For other divisions, see leaves 36 and 43-44.

tiers in *Love's Labour's,* in Prince Hal and in Cassio, but to the best advantage in some of the independent-minded ladies, especially in Rosalind, and above all, in Beatrice. Like Petruchio, she has seemingly embarked upon the task of curing the choler of her future spouse; but, being a woman, she uses methods more subtle and uses them before marriage rather than after. At first, Benedick is apparently inclined to ignore her; and, of all things, she will not be ignored. In the initial scene, she starts with a broadside of raillery against him: perhaps some of her sharp-tongued choler is assumed; but, if so, she is a good actress. The Prince thinks that the two would make an "excellent" match; but Leonato declares that "they would talke themselues madde"; and she is determined to burn out his choler with her own. The others trick her into believing that Benedick loves her, and trick Benedick into the same belief of her. She shrinks from being "condemn'd for pride and scorne so much"; and each grows more amenable to the other. She fears that someone will speak ill of her to Benedick, and so she must capitulate—but not too quickly; and so they woo, and plight their troth, though none too "peaceably"; and Burton, that shrewd physician of love malady, uses them as examples of choleric lovers: some there are (he says) "harsh and ready to disagree, offended with each other's carriage, like Benedick and Beatrice in the comedy, . . . by thus living together in a house . . . begin at last to dote insensibly one upon another."[112]   Thus choler can haply cure itself and justify a happy ending at the altar.

The varied symptoms of the choleric humor, Shakespeare repeatedly reflects. He follows current opinion in making it virile, brave, and given to anger; again and again, he associates it with heat and fire, with summer and youth, with the spleen, the liver, and the gall. In accordance with these concepts, Cassius is lean and martial heroes are handsome. Choler was thought to arise, not only from astral influence at birth, but also from temporal accidents such as age, hour, day, and season of the year, as reflected in *Romeo and Juliet,* from the

[112] Burton, III, 2, 2, 4. See the present writer, "Benedick and Beatrice," *cit. supra.*

accident or profession, as illustrated in Shakespeare's soldiers, from physical conditions of diet, as in *The Taming of the Shrew,* and of climate as in *Othello,* and especially from psychological causes such as wounded pride or envy of other men's good fortune, as shown in Hotspur and Iago. In an extreme form, it led to the ruin of all concerned, and might even bring catastrophe to the state; and thus Iago and Coriolanus, according to the Classical formula, progress from wounded pride to fury and so to revenge and ultimate disaster. In milder forms, tempered with self-control and some thought of others—for example, such sanguine-choleric figures under the influence of the sun as Henry V and Beatrice—it was the very humor for great ladies and great kings, who could be merciful and yielding as well as fierce or independent. Its quick wit gave brilliance of speech; but, in extreme cases, its ebullient emotions might bring irresponsible inconstancy. In short, it might illustrate the Golden Mean of Aristotle, good in proportion as it was moderate in quantity and power. All of these aspects of the choleric humor, Shakespeare sets forth not only in passing allusion, not only in vivid living examples like Hotspur, Olivia, and Claudio, but also in whole plays: in the jingo-chronicle *Henry V* that glorifies the victories of England, in comedies, *The Taming of the Shrew* and *Much Ado,* in which a pair of lovers overcome their choler and live happy ever after, in two great tragedies, *Othello* and *Coriolanus,* in which the clash of choleric wills brings all but universal ruin. Over and over, Shakespeare not only illustrates the action of this humor, but applies it by name to his choleric characters; and the critic who denies choler as an active force in motive and personality must, therefore, not only be blind to the choleric traits that these characters so amply set forth, but also be ready to accept the strange hypothesis that Shakespeare did not use an accepted Elizabethan word in its accepted Elizabethan sense. The only other possible conclusion is that Shakespeare actually does reflect this humor, and that such background, therefore, of contemporary psychology is fundamental in any historically just interpretation of his characters: *quod erat demonstrandum.*

CHAPTER V

THE MELANCHOLY TYPE

The humor of melancholy (black choler) is directly opposite the sanguine: it is cold and dry and therefore lacking in vitality and appropriate to age; it is painful to the sufferer and luckless in affairs. Quite properly, it is the furthest of the humors from the Aristotelian Mean; for such men were thought to oscillate, like sufferers today from manic-depressive psychosis, between a state of choleric violence that might run into madness, and a state of depressed, though by no means phlegmatic, quiet. It must not, therefore, be confused with the modern word *melancholy,* to which romanticism has given the sense of sweet passivity; and *The New English Dictionary* differentiates between the two. Elizabethan melancholy verged toward the abnormal; and yet Shakespeare does present a few figures, like Richard III and the bastard Edmund, who seem to be innately melancholy, and also a larger group in whom the humor has developed because of old age as in the senile Lear or because of some feeling or desire frustrated by the exigencies of life, as, for example, Orsino's unrequited love in *Twelfth Night,* or Hamlet's thwarted urge for revenge. In Shakespeare's works, moreover, the word *melancholy* occurs as noun or adjective some eighty times; and, indeed, the humor, being associated with the many ills that flesh is heir to, not only was common in Elizabethan popular literature but also supplied the subject for whole treatises such as Bright's, Ferrand's, and Burton's. This was the humor of thwarted but enduring passion; and, as such, it was proper to high tragedy, to *Hamlet* and to *Lear;* and it elsewhere appears in villains, in Shylock and in Don John in *Much Ado*. It is also the humor of religious mania—but dramatists avoided religion as a dangerous topic—and of disappointed lovers, like Romeo when he first enters moon-struck for the unattainable Rosaline. Melancholy and choler in their extremer forms belonged to social pariahs, to disinherited bastards like Edmund in *Lear,* to embittered younger brothers without future or fortune like the usurping dukes in *As You Like It* and *The Tempest*. Indeed, Orlando as a younger brother is particularly to be praised for keeping his honest sanguine nature despite the misfortune of his birth. A cripple like Richard III, a Moor like Aaron in *Titus Andronicus,* a Jew of the wicked usurer's trade like Shylock, all these are melancholic, all in revolt against established order, and therefore conspirators, usurpers, and villains. In short, melancholy was a parlous state big with the possibilities of drama.

Astrologically, as shown by Dariot[1] and Lemnius,[2] this humor was entirely under the evil and dangerous influence of Saturn. "Saturn is denominator" over the cunning Moor in *Titus;* Hal refers to the aging Falstaff as "Saturn," implying his amorous disability; and Conrade, who helps Don John in his wicked plot against Hero, was "born under Saturn." The humor was naturally associated with Saturday; and perhaps for this reason the charming Princess of France with her train of marriageable ladies leaves Navarre and so ends all the love affairs "On Saturday"; and Rosalind declares that she will love Orlando even on the unlucky days, "Fridays and Saturdays." The melancholy time of the year was appropriately autumn,[3] which, in *The Taming of the Shrew* and *Troilus,* Shakespeare associates with clouds and storms, and is therefore a proper season for the storm in *Lear*. Romeo and Juliet seem to have plighted their ill-omened troth in the melancholy afternoon.[4] Dariot describes this complexion as "Cold and dry . . . earthie, masculine, of the day, greatest misfortune.

---

[1] Dariot, sig. D 2 r. [2] Lemnius, leaf 146 v.
[3] *Ibid.*, leaf 135. [4] Vaughan, p. 126.

maleuolent, destroyer of life, slowe in effects, ponderous, waightie, terrible in all aspects. . . ." Elyot,[5] Clowes,[6] and Cuffe[7] also call it cold and dry and associate it with the alchemical element, earth. Shakespeare links cold with death and cowardice, and dryness with old age and its lack of the vital juices; and Romeo protests against "dry sorrow" as debilitating. Earth as an alchemical element is less clearly used in Shakespeare; but perhaps there is alchemical significance when Romeo spurns it as he climbs the wall of Juliet's garden, and so renounces his melancholy love for the obdurate Rosaline. The colors of black bile are fittingly listed in Dariot as "black, pale or wan, ashie," and the metals as "lead, black stones"; and Vicary describes the cheeks of a melancholic as "blowen in colour, and of little fleshe in substance."[8] Shakespeare in numerous passages associates black with sin and night, envy and evil, death and despair. Montague, concerned over his son's deep melancholy, declares:

> Black and portentous must this humor prove,
> Unless good counsel may the cause remove.

Twice in the same play, the color of ashes is used for a pale or deathlike complexion; and Romeo's unrequited love for Rosaline makes him "heavy" (Dariot called the humor "ponderous" and "waightie") so that he has "a soul of lead" and "cannot bound a pitch above dull woe." In fact, lead is the emblem for heaviness three times in the play; and Juliet describes "old folks" as "Unwieldy, slow, heavy and pale as lead." James I in his *Daemonologie,* a book that Shakespeare had reason to peruse,[9] discourses of melancholy men to distinguish them from witches:

For the humor of melancholie in the selfe is blacke, heauie and terrene, so are the symptomes thereof, in any persones that are subject therevnto, leannes, palenes, desire of solitude: and if they come to the highest degree thereof, mere folie and *Manie:* where

[5] Elyot, leaf 3 a.   [6] Clowes, p. 97.
[7] Cuffe, p. 97.   [8] Vicary, p. 41.
[9] See the present writer, *"Macbeth* as a Compliment to James I," *Eng. Stud.,* LXXII, 207 *et seq.*

as by the contrarie, a great nomber of them that euer haue bene convict or confessors of Witchcraft, as may be presently seene by manie that haue at this time confessed: they [witches] are by the contrarie, I say, some of them rich and worldly-wise, some of them fatte or corpulent in their bodies, and most part of them altogether giuen ouer to the pleasures of the flesh . . . which are thinges directly contrary to the symptomes of melancholie. . . .[10]

Hamlet aptly remarks that melancholy persons are especially predisposed to demonic influences.

The causes of melancholy were varied and complex. One might be born melancholy because of the ascendancy of Saturn at the time of birth, or because one was a Moor or a Jew or otherwise unfortunate.[11] Magistrates and students also were thought to be specially subject to it, for as Lemnius explains: "For through ouermuch agitatiõ of ye mynd, natural heat is extinguished, & ye Spyrits as well Animall as Vitall, attenuated and vanish away: whereby it cõmeth to passe, that after their vitall iuyce is exhausted, they fal into a Colde & Drye constitution."[12] Navarre and his court, perhaps because of the monastic tradition, clearly associate study with the austerities of a melancholy life. The Welsh schoolmaster in *Merry Wives* is pleased to exclaim upon his "melancholies." The jester Feste is not "lean enough to be thought a good student." The "churlish philosopher" Apemantus in *Timon of Athens* seems to be melancholy: one judges that Horatio, who is also a "scholar," had fortunately not studied long or hard enough at Wittenberg to have achieved these ill effects. Unnatural melancholy might arise from adustion, or burning out of the vitality; and though Shakespeare never mentions the word *adust,* he may have had the process in mind, for he repeatedly shows its two effects as set forth in Lemnius: the worst sort of unnatural melancholy, he says, "is compact and made of yealowe or yolkie Choler aduste. . . . If it be immoderatelye and too much enflamed, it bringeth the mynde into furious fitts, phrenticke rages, and brainsicke madnesse: Contrarylye,

[10] *Daemonologie,* p. 30; cf. Laurentius, pp. 98-99.
[11] Dariot, sig. D 2 r.   [12] Lemnius, leaf 135 v.

when all thinges consiste wythin mediocritye, it causeth and bringeth forth sharpnesse of witte, excellency of learning, subtility of inuentiõ, eloquence of tongue. . . ."[13]   Galen thought that certain foods caused melancholy, and various diets were proposed as cure; and the *General Practise of Medicine* ascribed as a cause for melancholy "studying without recreation or exercise of the body."[14]

The writers of the age do not always differentiate causes, symptoms, and effects of the disease; but melancholy certainly carried with it obvious psychological characteristics, which went with the humor, whether as cause or consequence. Burton imputes its rise generally to mental causes, as Shakespeare shows in Hamlet: ". . . most commonly, fear, grief, and some sudden commotion, or perturbation of the mind, begin it, in such bodies especially as are ill disposed."   One should calm these stormy passions and frustrated desires with the consolations of religion and philosophy; but most men, says Burton, "give all encouragement unto them."[15]   In *Much Ado,* the bastard Don John has rebelled against his brother, and has just been defeated and forgiven; but he is bitter and "out of measure sad":

I had rather be a canker in a hedge than a rose in his grace; and it better fits my blood to be disdained of all than to fashion a carriage to rob love from any: in this, though I cannot be said to be a flattering honest man, it must not be denied that I am a plain-dealing villain. I am trusted with a muzzle, and enfranchised with a clog; therefore I have decreed not to sing in my cage. If I had my mouth, I would bite; if I had my liberty, I would do my liking: in the meantime let me be that I am, and seek not to alter me.

The Elizabethans thought of melancholy persons as embittered, frustrated, "desirous of revenge";[16] they were apt at intrigue,[17] and, if given the power, were capable of managing the State";[18] and, like Richard III, they may by crooked means

---

[13] Lemnius, leaves 146 v and 147 r.   [14] I. M., sig. B 2 and 3.
[15] Burton, I, ii, 5, 4.
[16] Huarte, pp. 84-85.   [17] Walkington, p. 129.
[18] B. Riche, *My Ladies Looking-glasse* (London, 1616), p. 53.

achieve their high ambitions. Nashe compares a "brain oppressed with melancholy" to a "clocke tyde doune with too heavie weights."[19] Earle declared that a "High Spirited Man" whose hopes are contravened "turns desperately melancholy."[20]

Just such a man is Hamlet.[21] The Prince's natural humor, as he shows in his first talk with Rosencrantz and Guildenstern is sanguine; but the sudden death of his father and the dashing of his own immediate hopes for the crown by the marriage of his mother to Claudius, have made him bitter and melancholy at the beginning of the play: both Gertrude and the King mention this change in him, and hope that he may be brought again to his former merry self. Diverting recreation was an accepted treatment; and it might well have succeeded; for, as the King remarks, one does not forever mourn even for the most loved of fathers; and Claudius did his best to satisfy Hamlet's ambition by naming him Crown Prince. Then Hamlet heard the message of the Ghost; and a new frustrated passion troubled him: the obligation for revenge— or was it an obligation? How could he be sure that the apparition really was his father, and not, as some demonologists believed, the devil assuming this shape to make him commit the foul sin of regicide, and so bring his soul to hell? This doubt thwarts his fell purpose and augments his melancholy: he must devise some means to test the apparition's message. Meanwhile, his love for Ophelia must give way to higher things; and so it too is thwarted. Then the players come; and Hamlet has them give before the whole court a murder scene like that described by the Ghost. Claudius endures the test until Hamlet almost flings the accusation in his face; and then uses this insult as an excuse to leave the hall. At last, Hamlet is convinced, and declares that he will "take the Ghost's word for a thousand pound"; but he cannot sweep at once to his revenge, for he is sent to England; and the King, who has guessed from the play that Hamlet knows of the regicide, is

[19] T. Nashe, *Works,* ed. McKerrow, I, 357.

[20] Earle, *Microcosmographie.*

[21] See the present writer, *The "Hamlet" of Shakespeare's Audience* (Durham, N. C., 1938).

careful to keep him under guard. Melancholy has by degrees developed in the Prince a sense of intrigue: he has assured himself of the King's guilt, and he quickly extricates himself from the hands of his two traveling companions. On his return, he kills the King on the first good opportunity, at the fencing match with Laertes. His melancholy arises first from the death of his father and from frustrated ambition, then from frustrated revenge, and frustrated love; and, at the conclusion of the play, the revenge for his father is finally satisfied; his love and ambition have been swallowed up in stronger motives; and the violent forces that urged on the plot relapse to the quiescence of stable equilibrium. The tragedy is a perfect case-history of melancholy, not innate, but superinduced through psychological frustration.

One of the commonest causes of melancholy was disappointed love; Polonius and Rosalind both describe it; Jaques compares the sighing lover to a furnace; and Romeo's love for Rosaline is a "choking gall." Such an unsatisfied longing was thought especially to affect the pulse, according to the tradition of the *pulsus amatorious* which came down from the Alexandrian physician Erasistratus through Hippocrates and Galen to popular story in the *Gesta Romanorum* and Boccaccio:[22] Helena's secret love for Bertram affects her "pulse"; and, when Cressida is coming, Troilus declares:

> Even such a passion doth embrace my bosom:
> My heart beats thicker than a feverous pulse.

Ferrand and Burton treat of love melancholy at great length; and probably Shakespeare's fullest portrayal of it is the love-sick Duke Orsino in *Twelfth Night*.[23] He is by nature sanguine, and so of course is desperately in love with his charming neighbor who has recently fallen heiress to a title and great wealth. The lady, however, is at first too overwhelmed with the deaths of her father and her brother, which have left her

[22] See E. F. Horine, "An Epitome of Ancient Pulse Lore," *Bull. Hist. Med.,* X, 209 *et seq.*

[23] See the present writer, "The Melancholy Duke Orsino," *Bull. Hist. Med.,* VI, 1020 *et seq.*

in this state of parlous independence; and later she has, like Queen Elizabeth, become so enamored of this independence that she is not inclined to be enamored of any Duke who will certainly destroy it. Thus he sighs and sends messengers; and she will not hear the messages, and takes refuge in the deepest mourning. Lovesickness, "the Loveres maladye of hereos," as Chaucer called it, was a recognized disease in Greek, Arabic, and Mediæval medicine,[24] and in such poets as Theocritus and Dante. As explained by eminent authorities such as Boaistuau,[25] Burton,[26] and Ferrand,[27] and in such a popular work as Breton's *Melancholike Humours*,[28] Orsino's malady first entered his system through the eyes, and then progressed through "Liuer, Braine and Hart." Laurentius, likewise, declared that this type of melancholy started in the eyes and thereafter entered the liver, heart, and brain;[29] and Boaistuau declared that it proceeded from the eyes of the adorer to those of the adored and thence to the whole body; and he has even seen certain patients, "theire poore heart all burned, their Liuer and Lights all vaded and confumed, their Braines envomaged."[30] Burton lists the consequent torments of love,[31] and declares them greater than the tortures of the Inquisition; Bullein[32] and Laurentius[33] describe them as the "greatest misery." Orsino's disposition has become strangely unstable and "humorsome," and his "woes" include "groans that thunder love" and "sighs of fire." The lady, however, does not relent; and Orsino, finally rejected to his face, seeks consolation, as Romeo did, in a second choice, thus following the course of treatment advised by Burton[34] and Ferrand.[35] Apparently, he lives happy ever after; but, under less fortunate auspices, love melancholy could lead, as Polonius declares in *Hamlet,* to madness and desperate acts.

[24] See J. L. Lowes, "The Loveres Maladye of Hereos," *MP*, XI, 391 *et seq.*
[25] Boaistuau, pp. 192-193.
[26] Burton, III, 2, 2, 2; III, 2, 3; and III, 2, 5, 2.
[27] Ferrand, pp. 11-12, 41-42, 124.   [28] London, 1600, No. 21.
[29] Laurentius, p. 118.   [30] Boaistuau, pp. 202-203.
[31] Burton, III, 2, 1, 2.   [32] Bullein, leaves 25 v and 30 v.
[33] Laurentius, p. 119.   [34] Burton, III, 2, 5, 2.
[35] Ferrand, p. 257.

As the causes of melancholy were diverse, so were the types of the disease.[36] Laurentius explains:

> . . . there are many sorts of melancholie: there is one that is alto-
> gether grosse and earthie, cold and drie: there is another that is
> hot and adust, men call *atrabilis:* there is yet another which is
> mixed with some small quantitie of blood, and yet notwithstanding
> is more drie then moyst. The first sort which is grosse and earthie,
> maketh men altogether slacke in all their actions both of bodie and
> minde, fearefull, sluggish, and without understanding: it is com-
> monly called Asse-like melancholie: the second sort being hote and
> burnt, doth cause men to be outrageous and unfit to be imployed
> in any charge. There is none then but that which is mixed with a
> certaine quantitie of blood, that maketh men wittie, and causeth
> them to excell others.[37]

Nashe distinguishes two sorts of melancholy: the first, "Womens melancholy, which lasteth but for an houre"; but "the other . . . corrupteth all the blood, and is the cause of lunacie." Both are caused by "excessive studie," which thwarted natural bodily requirements, and are cured by "moderated recreations."[38] Elyot says that there are "two kyndes" of melancholy: "Natural which is the dregges of pure bloud, and is knowen by the blackness whã it issueth either downward or upwarde, and is verily colde and drye. Unnat-ural, whyche procedeth from the adustion of the colorik mix-ture, and is hotter and lighter, hauinge in it violence to kyll, with a daungerous disposition."[39] Bright, who was not quite orthodox, separates melancholy of the mind from that of the body, and subdivides the latter into natural and unnatural.[40] Lemnius says that unnatural melancholy is "farre worse and more pernicious"; for it is "blacke Melancholie"; he subdivides it into three types.[41] Huarte finds two species: "one naturall, which is the drosse of the bloud, whose temperature is cold and drie, accompanied with a substance very grosse, this serves not of any value for the wit, but maketh men blockish . . .

[36] Lemnius, leaf 147 v.   [37] Laurentius, pp. 85-86.
[38] Nashe, *Works, ed. cit.,* I, 357.   [39] Elyot, leaf 9 B.
[40] Bright, pp. 1-2.   [41] Lemnius, leaf 146 v.

because they want imagination. There is another sort, which is called *choler adust,* or *atra bile,* of which Aristotle said, That it made men exceeding wise." This last may be hot or cold, but is always dry.[42] To trace these various differentiations in Shakespeare's characters is somewhat difficult; but obviously Shakespeare makes distinctions, and the melancholy of Hamlet is of a less dangerous type than that of Richard III.

The physical symptoms of melancholy, set forth rather fully in Avicenna,[43] came down into Renaissance popular science. The humor, being the "dregs" of blood,[44] affected the whole body, and was the most "incommodious to health" of all physical states:[45] it hindered agility, and made the sufferer "very lecherous," like the wicked Edmund in *King Lear.* It might also cause stammering.[46] Among the "signes" of melancholy noted by Elyot are "Leannesse with hardnesse of skynne, Heare playne and thynne, Colour duskysh, or white with leannes."[47] Lemnius in general agrees, and lists, "body ill fauoured, leane dry, lank, pylde skinned and wythout hayre, . . . crooked . . . worne wyth sicknes and Oldage."[48] Bright says that the humor gives one a "leane, and spare body";[49] and Dariot also says, "leane, crooked, small eyes, thin beard, or none at all."[50] Of course, these characteristics generally fit old age as it appears in King Lear and in York in *Richard II;* they fit Hamlet's "lean beggar" and Jaques's "lean and slipper'd pantaloon," who needs "spectacles" and speaks in "childish treble"; and the "lean cheek" that Rosalind noted as an indispensable mark of love melancholy. Richard III, perhaps Shakespeare's best example of innate melancholy, is so misshapen that the dogs bark at him. Queen Margaret calls him:

> Thou elvish-marked, abortive, rooting hog!
> Thou that wast sealed in thy nativity
> The slave of nature and the son of hell!

[42] Huarte, pp. 84-85.
[43] Avicenna, *Libri in re medica omnes* (Venice, 1564), I, 428.
[44] Vaughan, p. 128.
[45] Lemnius, 135 r *passim.*
[46] Laurentius, p. 82.
[47] Elyot, leaf 3 a.
[48] Lemnius, leaf 146 r.
[49] Bright, pp. 154 *et seq.*
[50] Dariot, sig. D 2 r.

The obstruction of the liver with black bile brought on diseases;[51] and Dariot lists "trembling, black choller, palsies . . . coughes":[52] Shakespeare repeatedly associates palsy with melancholy dotage. Barrough adds tumors[53] and diseases of the eye[54]—a subject on which Laurentius wrote a whole disquisition. Dariot also mentions a "quartan," odd though it seems to link a fever with a cold damp humor: apparently, King John, who is melancholy in certain other respects, seems to die of such a fever; and, in *Antony and Cleopatra,* Enobarbus associates melancholy with "The poysonous dampe of night," which was thought to cause malaria. Several writers link this humor especially with the spleen;[55] and, though Shakespeare often seems to think this organ choleric, yet he also associates it with melancholy caprice, fits of passion and insanity, especially illustrated in King Lear. In short, writers generally blamed on melancholy most of the more serious diseases; and, as a result, a strange combination of physical symptoms was attributed to it.

The psychological symptoms are somewhat less confusing, although it is often hard to separate some types from extreme choler. Elyot, Bright, and Laurentius set forth the less violent, depressive aspects. Elyot says that melancholics sleep badly and have "fearefull" dreams; they have "Stiffe opinions," are "Tymerous and fearefull"; and their anger is "longe and fretting."[56] Bright says that they are subject to the wiles of Satan, and their "feare, doubt and distrust, stoppeth that consolation the mercy of God affordeth."[57] Laurentius adds that such men are "so cast downe and abase themselves, as that they become companions to the brute beasts, and have no pleasure to bee any where but in solitarie places"; indeed, a melancholy man is "one whom nothing can please, but onely discontentment which forgeth vnto it self a thousand false and vaine imaginations."[58] Even so King John, toward his unhappy

---

[51] Lemnius, leaf 141 v.   [52] Dariot, sig. D 2 r.
[53] Barrough, pp. 319, 346.   [54] *Ibid.,* p. 58.
[55] Dariot, sig. D 2 r; Lemnius, leaf 136 *passim.*
[56] Elyot, leaf 3 a.   [57] Bright, p. 249.
[58] Laurentius, pp. 81-82.

end, seems to "droop" and look "sad"; and the Bastard urges him:

> Let not the world see fear and sad distrust
> Govern the motion of a kingly eye.

Even the gay and licentious Iachimo is finally driven by his guilty conscience to a "heaviness" that "enfeebles" him. Indeed, *Cymbeline* is a play of melancholy types, the moody king, the treacherous queen, the unhappy princess reduced to last extremities, and her banished husband who "did encline to sadness, and oft-times Not knowing why." But the best example of this sort of melancholy is Timon after his loss of fortune.[59] The old-time virtue of liberality has been his ruin, and usurers have taken all his lands. Thus "The noblest mind ... That ever govern'd man" turns to bitterness, madness, and finally suicide. · He had been sanguine, becomes furiously choleric, and· this burns out to a deadly melancholy in which he cannot endure even the sight of men; and, as Laurentius puts it, he "becomes companion to the brute beasts." This seems a lame and impotent conclusion both for the hero and the play; but it is a perfect medical case-history.

Sometimes, melancholy expressed itself in a covetous cunning. Some items in Dariot suggest this type; but it is best set forth in Lemnius: ". . . churlish, whyning, wayward & ill to please, stubborne, intractable, obstinate, greedy of worldly goods, & couetous of money, pinching and sparing, whẽ they haue got it, & not daring to spẽd or bestow upon thẽselues such thinges as the necessity of mãs life for use requyreth."[60] This is an almost perfect characterization of Shylock, who objected to the amount his servant ate, and whose· house is described by· his daughter as "hell." Lemnius, furthermore, remarks that such are prone to "enuy, emulation, bitterness, hatred, spight, sorcery, fraude, subtlety, decepte, treason, sorrow, heauinesse, desperation, distrust and last of all to a lamẽ-

---

[59] See the present writer, "The Theme of 'Timon of Athens,' " *MLR*, XXIX, 20 *et seq.;* and "The Psychology of Shakespeare's Timon," *MLR*, XXXV, 521 *et seq.*

[60] Lemnius, leaf 146 r.

table and shameful end."[61]   And *The Merchant of Venice* leaves Shylock to just such a "shameful end."

The third is the most dangerous sort of melancholy. It is "ravenous" and "causeth imprisonments and secret enemies."[62] Huarte describes such men as "blasphemers, wily, double, friends of ill-doing; and desirous of revenge."[63] Walkington associates them with "dangerous Matchiavellisme."[64] When King John twice blames his murder of Prince Arthur on his "humor," there can surely be no question what that humor is; and, indeed, when he first approaches Hubert in the matter, he uses the *ipsissimum verbum:*

> . . . if the midnight bell
> Did, with his iron tongue and brazen mouth,
> Sound on into the drowsy ear of night;
> If this same were a churchyard where we stand,
> And thou possessed with a thousand wrongs;
> Or if that surly spirit, melancholy,
> Had baked thy blood and made it heavy-thick,
> Which else runs tickling up and down the veins,
> Making the idiot, laughter, keep men's eyes
> And strain their cheeks to idle merriment,
> A passion hateful to my pusposes; . . .
> Then, in despite of brooded watchful day,
> I would into thy bosom pour my thoughts. . . .

The play is a graphic picture of unprincipled politics, "Mad world! mad kings! mad composition!" The bastard Don John in *Much Ado,* who is "composed and framed of treachery" also illustrates this type of the humor; and perhaps best, or worst, of all, the bastard Edmund in *Lear.* Illegitimate offspring, being outcasts unless fully recognized by their fathers, were expected to be evil and therefore melancholy;[65] and Edmund, who has traveled abroad and learned Italianate cunning, illustrates "villanous melancholy." He will, "if not by birth, have lands by wit." He betrays first his brother, then his

---

[61] *Ibid.,* leaf 23 v.   [62] Dariot, sig. D 2 v.
[63] Huarte, p. 147.   [64] Walkington, p. 129.
[65] See the present writer, "Bastardy in Shakespeare's Plays," *Sh. Jhb.,* LXXIV, 123 *et seq.*

father, becomes the lover of both queens, and betrays them to each other: he is the super-villain of a play of horrors. In the end, he declares, "some good I mean to do, Despite of mine own nature"; and he tries to save the lives of Lear and Cordelia, but in vain.

This type of melancholy especially fits the "heavy villain"; and Richard III is another excellent example, the younger son of a younger son, deformed and wickedly cunning: the Lady Anne calls him a "Foul devil"; and he compares himself to "Iniquity," and admits his "naked villany," outwardly clothed "With old odd ends stolen out of holy writ." Richard is in fact what critics have miscalled Iago, but he lacks Iago's overwhelming motives. As he declares in his first soliloquy, he revels in gratuitous villainy; he deceives character after character, and, under the guise of friendship, lures each to disgrace and death: the royal father and the husband of Lady Anne, the Dukes of Clarence and Buckingham, Lords Hastings, Rivers and Grey, and Sir Thomas Vaughan, and, above all, the Princes in the Tower, King Edward V and his brother. This is a carnival of Machiavellian death and destruction. Of course, any loyal subject of the House of Tudor had to picture as monster and tyrant the King whom Elizabeth's grandfather had killed at Bosworth Field and supplanted on the throne; and Shakespeare's play, like Sir Thomas More's biography, thoroughly blackened Richard's character, so that at the end, we may heave a conscientious sigh of relief at the coronation of the illegitimate Tudor as King Henry VII. Shakespeare depicts Richard Crookback as innately melancholy; he is as bad as he can be at the beginning, and so goes through no psychological evolution: he is a vitalized personified evil of the old morality drama.

Melancholy often carried its own retribution in consequent lunacy. Such a popular author as Nashe explains that spirits of the earth and water, "feeding on foggie-braind melancholly, engender thereof many vncouth terrible monsters," and thus the mind is finally "distracted" and "destroyed."[66] Overbury,

---

[66] Nashe, *ed. cit.*, I, 353 *et seq.*

likewise, describes a melancholy man as one whom a "crazed disposition has altered."[67]   Such have dreams by night and strange fantasies by day; and Lemnius,[68] Walkington,[69] and Laurentius[70] cite edifying cases.   Just so Richard III has a "fearful dream" just before the Battle of Bosworth Field; and Shylock, just before the elopement of Jessica, "did dream of money-bags," and so is "loath" to leave his house; and in King John's last illness, he has "many legions of strange fantasies." Mercutio fears that Romeo's love melancholy will unbalance his mind; and the unhappy Lady Constance, mother of Prince Arthur, "in a franzy died"; and Lear, whose choleric humor dries to melancholy with old age and mental shock, becomes raving mad.[71]   James I had declared that melancholy leads to utter insanity and "manie";[72] and Shakespeare in *Lear,* which seems to have been calculated closely to the meridian of the royal taste, shows this disintegration by nice degrees: even at the beginning of Act I, the old man begins to fear for his sanity; in Act II, he feels himself succumbing to *hysterica passio,* and begs Goneril, "do not make me mad"; in Act III, his "wits begin to turn," and he feels the "cold" of the storm, a suggestion that the heat and dryness of choler are no longer strong in him; finally, late in the act, his "wits are gone"; and, in Act IV, he is "mad as the vext sea."   According to medical tradition, derived from Galen's *De Pulsibus,* moreover, an irregular pulse was a sign of lunacy; and, in *The Comedy of Errors,* Pinch wants to feel Dromio's pulse to test his sanity; and Hamlet, in the famous closet scene, offers the same test to his mother:

> My pulse, as yours, doth temperately keep time,
> And makes as healthful music: it is not madness
> That I have utter'd.

[67] T. Overbury, *Characters,* "Melancholy Man."
[68] Lemnius, leaf 150 *et seq.*   [69] Walkington, chap. xiii.
[70] Laurentius, pp. 100 *et seq.*
[71] See the present writer, "The Old Age of King Lear," *JEGP,* XXXIX, 527 *et seq.*
[72] James I, *op. cit.,* p. 30; and Batman, pp. 32-33.

This would have been sound proof (if proof were needed) to the Elizabethan audience that Hamlet was not insane, as some critics have believed.

Although, unnatural melancholy might make one "Doltish,"[73] or a man of "few woords,"[74] and cause "dullnesse of conceit,"[75] yet some sorts might make one very witty.[76] According to James I, melancholy persons were talkative;[77] and, on the unimpeachable authority of Aristotle, Walkington allowed them "most dexterical wits," though "shallow reason,"[78] and Vaughan allowed them both wit and a "deeper understanding" than others.[79] For this reason, the humor became an elegant affectation, "the Creast of Courtiers Armes"[80] and very "gentlemanlike,"[81] and the proper style for the fine and traveled Jaques. Richard III cleverly copes in repartee even with the outraged Lady Anne; and Hamlet bandies wit with all comers—Rosencrantz, Guildenstern, Polonius, and Ophelia. How far these melancholy characters of Shakespeare had the "deeper understanding" that Aristotle and his followers allowed them depends on one's attitude toward the cynical philosophy of Richard and Jaques and on one's belief in Hamlet as a philosopher.[82]

The cures for melancholy properly combined physical and mental therapy. Since diet was thought to be a cause of the distemper, diet, as in choler, was an obvious mode of treatment, suggested by Boorde,[83] Barrough,[84] Laurentius[85] and others: in *Richard III,* the old King Edward IV is described as "sickly, weak and melancholy" from "evil diet"; and Iago craves to "diet" his revenge, that is to feed it adequately and so to cure it. Boorde advises a melancholy man to avoid wines; but Lemnius thinks them at least sometimes medicinal;[86] and

[73] Lemnius, leaf 148 v.
[74] Dariot, sig. D 2 r.
[75] Bright, pp. 157-159.
[76] Huarte, pp. 84-85.
[77] James I, *op. cit.,* p. 30.
[78] Walkington, pp. 111, 128-129.
[79] Vaughan, p. 128.
[80] Lyly, *Midas,* V, ii, 104.
[81] Jonson, *Every Man in His Humor,* I, iv.
[82] See the present writer, *The "Hamlet" of Shakespeare's Audience* (Durham, N. C., 1938), pp. 197-198.
[83] Boorde, ed. *EETS,* Ex. Ser. X, 289.
[84] Barrough, p. 59.
[85] Laurentius, p. 104.
[86] Lemnius, leaf 138 v.

Falstaff's heavy drinking is perhaps an effort to counteract the melancholy of his advancing years, and maintain the vitality of youth.[87]   Since sedentary study was sometimes a cause, Bright advises moderate exercise;[88] and the elegantly melancholy Don Armado takes exercise to cure his affected melancholy.   Laurentius urges music;[89] and this contributes to Lear's short recovery; and Orsino and Cleopatra when Antony goes to Rome, call for music, though there was some doubt how much good it did to lovers.   Sleep was a more generally accepted treatment;[90] and this undoubtedly helped Lear.   After discussing these physical cures, Burton takes up the psychological, and urges relief from perturbations and discontents.[91] Lemnius advises that one both "cherrishe" the body and relieve "that inconvenience which distēpereth the minde."[92]   For this purpose, diversions, games, and "Moderate myrthe and banqueting" were prescribed.[93]   Twice in *The Comedy of Errors,* recreation is advised as a cure for the complaint:

> Sweet recreation barr'd, what doth ensue
> But moody and dull melancholy.

Benvolio proposes to mitigate Romeo's love melancholy by diversions, and so induces him to go to the Capulet ball. Polonius and Gertrude hope that "delights" and the merry company of his college friends will bring Hamlet back to his wonted self.   In *The Winter's Tale,* the King goes to the ocean "to purge melancholy."   Shakespeare, in short, reflects not only the causes, the symptoms, and the progress of melancholy but also its accepted cures; but, in violent cases such as Richard III or Lear, there was no cure.

The present chapter is not a complete discussion of melancholy.   Elizabethans, in both learned and popular style, wrote more, and more diversely, on this humor than on any other, perhaps because its effects were more morbid and therefore

---

[87] See Ruth E. Sims, "The Green Old Age of Falstaff," *Bull. Hist. Med.,* XIII, 144 *et seq.*   [88] Bright, pp. 302-303.
[89] Laurentius, p. 104.   [90] Lemnius, leaf 152 r.
[91] Burton, II, 3, 1.   [92] Lemnius, leaf 145 r.
[93] *Ibid.,* leaf 154 v; Bright, pp. 300 *et seq.;* Nashe, *ed. cit.,* I, 257; S. Guazzo, *The Civile Conversation* (London, 1925), I, 18 *et seq.*

more apparent; and several extended treatises are devoted entirely to it. The aim of the present study has been to set forth briefly the chief features, most of which Shakespeare reflects, and to illustrate these features with enough reference to the plays to show how Shakespeare used them. Melancholy supplied many of the villains and some of the wits of the contemporary stage; and, if Shakespeare had presented more of the religious and more of the elderly types, the number of his melancholy characters would be much greater; but religion was a dangerous topic and drama generally has to do with young, or at least vigorous, people. In fact, most of Shakespeare's melancholy characters are not naturally so, but have acquired the complaint through disappointed love or like misfortune; and therefore they are presented as only partly melancholy, or as melancholy only for the time: if Hamlet had not died, he doubtless would later have regained his sanguine self as Duke Orsino did. But the humor was too violent to run to happy endings; and Lear and Edmund come to ruin and drag down with them the entire state.

Caliban is the melancholic temper untrammeled by even so much humanity as King John or Richard III or Edmund was possessed of: like Timon, he is a man reverted to the beasts; and, indeed, just as Ariel is an alchemical spirit of the air, so Caliban personifies the dull and drossy element of earth. He is the son of "This damn'd witch Sycorax," who was given to rash and "unmitigable rage." He is "A fleckled whelp hag-born—not honor'd with a human shape," like Richard Crookback; and he first enters with a curse. He illustrates many of the melancholy traits; he is "laborious"[94] for Prospero; his mind is "doltish,"[95] for he mistakes the drunken Stephano for a god, and finally has to call himself "a thrice-double ass"; like Edmund, he is "lecherous,"[96] for he had tried to force Miranda to his lust; like King John, he has fantastic visions; and, like Lear, lapses "into madness." Above all, he is a "most

[94] Dariot, sig. D 2 r.
[95] Lemnius, leaf 148 v.
[96] Ibid., leaf 135 r.

lying slave, Whom stripes may move, not kindness." He calls
on all the earthy infections "From bogs, fens, flats" to light on
Prospero's head; and he conspires with Stephano and Trinculo
to murder his good master. As Hamlet remarks, melancholy
was thought to make one subject to demonic agencies: it is,
moreover, certainly Caliban's elemental humor and probably
that of the Witches in *Macbeth;* and, indeed, it was the proper
complexion for "Hag-seed" of "vile race."

CHAPTER VI

THE BALANCED AND THE MERCURIAL TYPES

The Elizabethans thought of an individual's body (and therefore of his mind) as generally ruled by a single fluid; but they recognized also the possibility of a combination of the humors, a combination that might result in the perfect balance of physical and mental health, or might, on the contrary, express the weak instability of the mercurial complexion. Both of these states seem to have been regarded as rare, for some contemporary treatises ignore them, and Shakespeare seems to illustrate them in only a few of his characters. The perfect balance, moreover, like the phlegmatic humor was too impassive and static to be of great dramatic use; and the mercurial would generally be appropriate only to wavering and talkative persons such as the Elizabethans would probably despise. In short, these two combinations of the humors were likely to produce an extreme of solid worth or of unstable weakness.

Astrologers, such as Dariot, give no consideration to the perfect balance of the humors: how could one be born when all the planets and contellations were at once in the ascendant? Medicine also, treating of diseases rather than of health, says little of the perfectly balanced man. The proportions of the balance, moreover, need not be equal; for Lemnius thought that two parts of blood should be proportioned to one each of bile (choler) and black bile.[1] To make matters more difficult, this happy condition in its psychological effects easily confuses

[1] Lemnius, leaf 100 r.

with the sanguine type; and, indeed, the main distinction between them consists in the weaknesses to which the latter was
exposed: love in extreme and violent forms, and deceit on the
part of others. The former misfortune shows Orlando and
the noble Angelo sanguine rather than balanced; the latter
puts Brutus and Duncan, the exiled Duke in *As You Like It*
and Prospero in the same category. In the end Prospero perhaps achieved perfect poise of mind and body, but he did not
have it when he gave so much time to study that he neglected
the government of Milan and so was deceived and cast out by
his brother.[2] In that age of physical violence and choleric
passions when the restraints and Aristotelian ideals of Classical
education affected but a few, a balanced personality, as Lemnius remarks, was indeed a rare phenomenon:

. . . the life of man is subiect euery where & in all places to innu-
merable casualties, myssehapps and inconueniencies, and is on ech
syde beset & torne in peeces wyth suche a number of myseryes and
by reckenyngs, as euery way weaken and appayre the perfect vigoure
and lustye state thereof. But if no myschaunce or harme assault
the same, it may in good case & temper many yeares continue: as
by frugality, holesome diet, & orderly qualification of all affections:
insomuche that euen till the yeares of decrepicie, there doe appeare
the tokens and markes, of a righte good Constitution and habite:
which thing is manifestlye to bee seene by some that in Oldage are
as lusty, and haue their wittes as freshe and youthlyke, and their
bodyes not so barreine, unactiue & fruitlesse, as many Yong men
haue.[3]

Jean Fernel, physician to Henry II of France, even declared
that such a perfect balance was unattainable.[4]

Hill seems to be referring to the balanced type when he
says that average stature should go with a comely appearance,
a "wittie" mind, and an "honest" character;[5] and Lemnius
attributes to this happy medium all possible excellencies, in
contrast to the extremes of melancholy:

---

[2] See the present writer, "Political Themes in Shakespeare's Later Plays," *JEGP*,
XXXV, 61 *et seq.*   [3] Lemnius, leaf 94 v.
   [4] Sir Charles Sherrington, *Man on His Nature* (Cambridge, 1941), p. 18.
   [5] Hill, leaf 126 v.

Such a one therefore as we do here shadow out and dexcribe, is in heart and mynd so well settled and perfectly stayed, that he is not to be drawē to either party, or to wauer and totter this way and yᵗ way, but perseuereth still in one stay of stedfastnes & cōstancy, without any kind of alteration or mutibility. In him there are (in deede) affectiōs, but yet such as bee natural & not discōmendable, as, loue and jealous affectiō to his wife, Childrē and such as hee wisheth wel unto, whom as hee doth not fondly cocker and suffer to runne at random, or to haue the full scope of theyr owne wanton wils: so againe, is he not to thē bitter, strait, rigorous, spightful, wayward nor stubborn, but so, that in familiar communication and company with them, he useth a gentle mildnes, seasoned wt an earnest and reuerend grauity, wythoute much prattling & tattling, wythout byting skoffes, & upbrayding tauntes, wtout al uncomrly and unciuil iestinge, pleasauntlye conceyted, and meerye wyth honestye, not using therein anye filthynes or rybauldrye: and as hee is moste farre of from all malapert scurrility and scenicall gesture, so is he againe most farre from sulleyne sterne seuerity, & from Stoicall indolency. . . .

And not onely in the inward mynd of man, do these ornamentes and giftes of nature appeare & expresselye shew out themselues, but euen in the outward shew, shape and behauiour of the bodye there is euidētly descryed and perceyued a comely grace and portlye dignity. For in the countenaunce, whych is the image of the minde, in the eyes, which are the bewrayers and tokentellers of the inward conceiptes: in the colour, lineamentes, proportion and feacture of the whole bodye, there appeareth a kinde of heroicall grace and amyablenes, insomuch that the very viewe & sighte thereof, allureth and draweth euery one by a certayne secrete sympathie or cōsent of Nature to loue it, wythout any hope of profite or commodity thereby to bee reaped or receyued. The body is decently made & featly framed, conteyninge an absolute construction and comely frame of al the parts together. The head not aslope cornered, but rounde and globewyse fashioned, the hayre of fayre aburne or chesten colour: the forhead smoth, cheerefull and unwrynckled, beautifyd wyth comely eyebrowes, and greatly honoured wyth a paire of amyable eyes, not holow, but delightfully standing out. The colour freshe, sweete and pleasaunte. The cheekes and the balles thereof steygned and dyed in a perfect hew of whyte and redde, and that naturally, speciallye in the lusty yeares of Adoles-

cencie. The porte & state of the body bolt uprighte, the gate or
goinge framed to comelynes, not nycely affected nor curiously
counterfaicted, as it were Players & disguysed Masquers, who by a
kinde of upstarte & stately gate, hopeth the rather to winne credite,
estimation and authority, and to be made more accompte of,
amonge the common people. The tongue prompy and ready, dis-
tinctly and sensibly able to pronounce and deliver out hid meaning,
in wordes of gallant utteraunce.[6]

Shakespeare seems to present but one indubitable example
of the perfectly balanced type, the young Danish scholar
Horatio. *Hamlet* is a drama of physical and emotional violence and of frustrated wills and passions that now and again
burst out of all control. Hamlet himself is a very star incandes-
cent from inner pressure to the point of explosion; his pent-up
feelings have turned his natural sanguine self to the opposite
extreme of melancholy, which he expresses in a series of great
soliloquies. As this inner vehemence grows, he comes to value
more and more the serenity of perfect poise; and, more and
more, he turns to the unmoved Horatio, sympathetic yet calm
and reposeful, the complete opposite of his own spiritual tur-
bulence; and their slight acquaintance at college ripens into a
deep friendship.[7] Thus, to offset by contrast the psychology
of the Prince, Horatio is dramatically outlined in his immediate background, the man of perfect balance in a crashing
world.

Horatio himself does even less in the play than he does in
some earlier versions of the story, but the dialogue brings out
his nicety of poise. At first, he hardly believes that his friend
Marcellus has seen an actual ghost, and thinks "'twill not
appear"; but he is willing to "hear Bernardo speak of this."
Suddenly, the Ghost reveals itself, and he is harrowed "with
fear and wonder"; but even this does not break down his outward calm, and he has the presence of mind to address the
apparition in proper terms and charge it to speak. It vanishes,
and Horatio is puzzled why it came. The three discuss the

---

[6] Lemnius, leaf 35 v, *passim.*

[7] See the present writer, *The "Hamlet" of Shakespeare's Audience* (Durham,
N. C., 1938), esp. chaps. ii and x.

preparations for war then going on; and Horatio is in the midst of a lecture on omens when suddenly the Ghost returns, and he at once improvises a sort of incantation to make it stay and speak; but again it vanishes. At Horatio's suggestion they inform Hamlet in the following scene of this strange visitation, and arrange for him to watch the following night. Horatio was brought in as having the education (he is a "scholar") and good sense to address the Ghost properly; and he has acquitted himself well. From this point on, he is seen merely in the background of the court or in the company of the Prince, and so of course has little to say before such exalted persons. He has the presence of mind to object to Hamlet's going off with the Ghost alone, for the Ghost might indeed be a devil and injure him; but the later great events of the tragedy but slightly ruffle his calm: at Hamlet's request he watches Claudius during the play, and reports on his impressions afterwards; he does not exclaim at the Prince's unexpected return from the voyage to England; he sees Hamlet and Laertes wrestle in Ophelia's grave, barely comments at the deaths of Rosencrantz and Guildenstern, warns Hamlet against the fencing match but watches it in silence, and speaks a brief epitaph at his friend's death. He is a silent chorus, an influence seen and felt but scarcely an actor in the tragedy. Hamlet remarks on his serenity and gives it as the reason for their growing friendship: first, the Prince calls him the most balanced ("just") man he has ever known, and then goes on to praise Horatio because his passions and reason are so perfectly in tune that he has true self-control:

> Since my dear soul was mistress of her choice,
> And could of men distinguish, her election
> Hath seal'd thee for herself: for thou hast been
> As one, in suffering all, that suffers nothing;
> A man that fortune's buffets and rewards
> Hast ta'en with equal thanks: and blest are those
> Whose blood and judgement are so well commingled
> That they are not a pipe for fortune's finger
> To sound what stop she please. Give me that man

That is not passion's slave, and I will wear him
In my heart's core, ay, in my heart of heart,
As I do thee.

This is the key to Horatio's character. He represents calm
and sanity in a play of madness and horrors. With cool ob-
jectivity, even in the tense scene following the play-within-the-
play, he criticizes his friend's extempore stanza, and later does
not hesitate to tell him that he will lose the fencing match.
He is the perfect complement to the sanguine enthusiast whom
sorrow and prolonged duress have turned to melancholy; and
his presence doubtless helps Hamlet to that politic restraint
that circumstances required. For a man of Horatio's moderate
status, born without wealth or noble friends, this experience
as close associate of his Prince was a tremendous thing; and
yet he never shows conceit or silliness like the favorites of
Edward II in Marlowe's play. At Hamlet's death, for a moment his spirit wavers, and he would follow his Prince; but,
at Hamlet's plea, he pauses, and so lives to explain the "carnal,
bloody and unnatural acts" to Fortinbras, "lest more mischance
On plots and errors happen." He could not bring Hamlet
peace, but perhaps he can bring it to Denmark. He is a
Prospero who does not break his staff.

Here and there elsewhere in the plays, one glimpses this
same balanced serenity of personality. Perhaps the flawless
Sebastian in *Twelfth Night,* who caps his romantic career by
wedding the Countess-heroine of the comedy, is a case in point.
Perhaps the jocular Prince, Don Pedro in *Much Ado,* is an
example. He is gracious and tactful and yet merry, and, un-
like most of the sovereigns in the earlier plays, has a major
part in the plot; in fact, he acts as marriage-broker in both
the love affairs. He can bandy wit even with Benedick until
the latter cries, "Nay, mock not, mock not." This "Sweet
prince" can rise to almost any occasion, can evade a quarrel
with Leonato, can pay back Dogberry in his own clipped coin;
but the fact that he is so easily deceived about Hero's virtue
suggests that he belongs with Duncan rather to the sanguine
type than to the balanced personality.

A likelier candidate, perhaps is Gonzalo, the "Honest lord" in *The Tempest*. Like Polonius, he has the dry wit and something of the aphoristic bent of age.[8] He had saved Prospero and Miranda when they were set adrift by the wicked usurper, and had given them "necessaries" and the "books" that made Prospero's magic possible. He is introduced as the only calm person on the breaking ship, and he can even indulge in an ironic comment on the Boatswain's "complexion." Like Sir Thomas More, he has notions of an ideal commonwealth "To excel the golden age." He is the only one who has the presence of mind when they are safe ashore to note that the salt water has not spoiled their clothes, and so he seems to have an inkling that the storm was something more than natural. Prospero greets him with a high regard like that Hamlet used to Horatio:

> First, noble friend,
> Let me embrace thine age, whose honour cannot
> Be measured or confined.

At the end, Gonzalo blesses the two lovers, and points out how happily for all concerned the episodes have transpired. Like Horatio, he has little part in the plot; but, also like Horatio, he stands as a contrasting symbol of benign sanity, unshaken by storms, misadventures, and enchantments.

The mercurial type is somewhat commoner, but also is limited to special dramatic uses. Like the phlegmatic type, it shows pliability rather than strength of character, and so was unsuited to persons in great place: the complexion, therefore, appears at its best in such comic figures as Moth, Mercutio, and Feste; and, in Richard II and Macbeth, it results in catastrophe. Named after the planet Mercury, this type is mainly astrological; and Dariot, therefore, is the chief contemporary source for information: he describes it as "Of mutable nature, good with good and badde with bad pla[nets] and so is he masc. or fem. fortunate or infortunat hot or cold, moyste or dry, according to the planets to whom he is ioyned, but of hys

---

[8] See C. R. Sleeth, "Shakespeare's Counsellors of State," *Rev. Anglo-Amèr.*, XIII, 97 *et seq.*

owne nature colde and drye: long fingers, of a doubtfull nature, alwaies imagining newe things, not taking rest. . . ." He
associates it with gray or "mixt" colors and with quicksilver,
with the "memory, tongue, fantasie . . . hands, fingers, gall,
bones, thighes, sinewes, of the brayne"; and it was prone to
"madnes . . . lethargie, doting, stammering impediments of
the tongue, hoarcenes, the falling sicknes, coughes . . . vomit
. . . and all melancholy diseases."[9]   Dr. Arcandam notes also
that such men have hair on the chest and are of light flesh.[10]

Here and there, Shakespeare seems to reflect one or more
of these astrological and physical details in his mercurial characters.   The caddish philanderer Proteus in *Two Gentlemen*
in both his name and actions suggests the complexion.   Mercutio, whose name also suggests this humor, has "dancing shoes
with nimble soles," and is killed on Monday afternoon, a
phlegmatic weekday and a melancholy hour.   Although the
Nurse in *Romeo and Juliet* by sex and social status should be
phlegmatic, yet perhaps age has made her cold and dry and
so mercurial: at all events, her lucky hours and her garrulous
tongue suggest as much.[10a]   Certainly Wednesday, which was
thought a mercurial day, produces violent reversals of plot in
Romeo and Juliet.   Julius Caesar, as Shakespeare portrays him,
seems mercurial: he has the "falling sicknes," is given to fantasies and superstition, and is so cold and dry that he had not
the vitality to swim the Tiber like the choleric Cassius.   Ober-
on's jester and factotum, the lightsome Puck, seems to be
mercurial in his impish moods and lightning transformations,
"Like horse, hound, hog, bear, fire, at every turn"; and that
other chameleon entertainer, the jester Feste, is not "lean," and
perhaps his technique of constant change arises both from his
art and from his nature.   Cleopatra seems to consider herself
a variable mixture of chemical "elements": "I am Fire, and
Ayre; my other Elements I giue to baser life."   The thief
Autolycus in *The Winter's Tale* imputes his crafty roguery to
his being "littered under Mercury."[11]   The "braine-sickly"

[9] Dariot, sig. D 4 v-E 1 r.   [10] Arcandam, sig. L 7-8.
[10a] See "Juliet's Nurse" by A. Guido, *Bull. Hist. Med.,* about to appear.
[11] See Christine White, "A Biography of Autolycus," *Sh. Assoc. Bull.,* XIV, 158
et seq.

Macbeth changes his feelings and his purposes with the company he keeps; his "hands fingers, bones, thighes, sinewes" are so well developed that his "brandisht Steele" can cleave Macdonwald at one stroke, and incontinently dispatch young Seward. But in all these characters, the physical details are merely incidental to matters of social plane and especially of character.

According to Dariot, the mercurial complexion was appropriate to students of "Mathematick, rhetorick, philosophy," to those who affect elegance in writing and "the magistery of arts." Such would be clever talkers, wits, and entertainers, a page like the "volable" Moth in *Love's Labour's,* a courtier like the loquacious Mercutio, a jester like the irrepressible Feste, and that past-mistress of all sport and diversion, the incomparable Cleopatra, who, like the others, though on a more exalted plane, lived by her wits. Such were "merchants, inuentors of subtle arts. Among the lower orders, the complexion appertains to younger brothers, "seruants, scribes, grauers, ingenious workmen in euerye thinge." Such men, in short, as depended more on wit than on character, and could turn and turn as Othello falsely accused his Desdemona: in a rogue, a page, or a jester, that might be well enough, and might avail a woman like Cleopatra, but it would hardly fit the royal status of Richard II or Macbeth.

In character, Dariot finds the type "ingenious, wayward, wauering, violent, not seldome mournefull, inconstant, lyars, proud . . . crafty, instable. . . ." Hill agrees that Mercury makes men ingenious;[12] and Adams discusses the more theological aspects: such men have mental inconstancy and physical vertigo; like Macbeth, they "would come to heauen" but for their "halting"; their "affections" are "but a little lukewarm water"; and "In a controuerted point" such an one "houldes with the last reasoner hee has either heard or read. . . ." This weakness "proceeds from cloudy imaginations, fancies, fictions, and forced dreames, which keepe the mind from a sober and peaceful considerateness."[13] Religion is the only cure.

---

[12] Hill, leaf 50 v.   [13] Adams, pp. 7 *et seq.*

Probably the first full portrait that Shakespeare drew of the mercurial type is his Richard II. Holinshed's Richard, although displaying a somewhat bewildering variety of humors, does not particularly show the vacillation of the mercurial temper; and Marlowe's *Edward II,* on which Shakespeare seems somewhat to have modeled his plot, presents, not a mercurial, but a luxurious and phlegmatic king. This interpretation of Richard, therefore, is Shakespeare's own; and he develops the psychological aspects of mercury with reiterated insistence, so that Richard, as he himself declares, is "in one person many people." At his first appearance, he vacillates as arbiter in the quarrel between Bolingbroke and Mowbray. Though the two brand each other as traitors and liars, though Mowbray scorns any patchwork peace, though Richard sees that both are "In rage deaf as the sea, hasty as fire," yet he repeatedly insists that they "purge this choler without letting blood." He entreats them weakly, and at long last sets a date for the trial-by-combat at Coventry. At this trial, he has sworn to be "impartial," but publicly shows preference for Bolingbroke. Moreover, when the contestants have taken their oaths and are ready, he suddenly forbids the trial, and dooms Bolingbroke to ten years' exile and Mowbray to exile for life. He rejects the latter's plea for clemency, but, even unasked, at once commutes Bolingbroke's lighter sentence to "six winters," though he fears Bolingbroke's popularity and wishes that he might never return. Thus the flaccid King breaks his every pledge. In Act IV, the choleric Bolingbroke settles a similar trial in two and a half lines.

Richard's vacillation is the repeated keynote of the play. At the first sign of disaster, he turns on his dear favorites, unreasonably accuses them of treachery, and declares that "their heads shall pay for it." He cannot make up his mind whether to try to placate Bolingbroke or try to fight him, and so does neither and becomes a prisoner without a blow. He will "be contented" to renounce the crown and have "an obscure grave"; but he wavers in his abdication, and answers Bolingbroke, "Ay, no; no, aye." He confesses his faults with extravagant remorse, and yet still thinks himself a Divine

Right King, and whines at the retribution visited on him. In short, he is at first the sanguine monarch with "youth at the prow and pleasure at the helm," with something of sanguine charm, and of phlegmatic love of luxury; then for a time, he is the choleric soldier in the Irish wars and later at his death; but most of the latter acts show him immersed in sentimental melancholy, bemoaning his fate with lyrical hyperboles, torn between extravagant boasting and a groveling despair, which he finds "sweet." Well might the Bishop of Carlisle somewhat caustically remark:

> My lord, wise men ne'er sit and wail their woes,
> But presently prevent the ways to wail.

He repeatedly compares himself to Christ, insults the nobles in whose power he is, and in the same breath admits his "weaved-up folly." Indeed, he could not be more foolish, weak, and impolitic. Of course, the conclusion is stark tragedy; for such an one, especially in that age of iron, could not hold fast the turbulent reins of rule.[14]

Such also is Julius Caesar, portrayed in his weak old age. Such also is Macbeth, whom critics have found so contradictory and difficult. He actually has the vacillation so commonly attributed to Hamlet. His stronger wife calls him "Infirme of purpose" and subject to the fantasies of "Child-hood." She declares that his "Constancie" has left him "vnattended." His mind is "full of Scorpions"; and he doubts decisions even in the making. Without Lady Macbeth, he would not have killed the King and yet would have regretted not doing so; and he puts off the murder of Macduff until too late and then blames his "flighty purpose." His shifting character confuses not only modern critics but also the characters about him in the play: he was an "honest" soldier, is now a cruel "Tyrant"; some think him "Mad"; some, "valiant"; indeed, "His pester'd Senses . . . recoil and start." Toward the end, he seems to realize that he has a "minde diseased," demands a physician, and then cries hopelessly, "Throw Physicke to the dogs, Ile none of it." In the camp, he is brave and choleric; before Duncan, sanguine and jovial; with his wife, subtle and treach-

---

[14] C-- the present writer, "Richard II," PQ, XXI, 228 et seq.

erous; he is the true son of Mercury, "mutable . . . good with
the good, euill with the euill." Miss Campbell thinks him
fearful and so presumably phlegmatic;[15] but he is not afraid
in the fighting either at the beginning of the play or at the
end; his humor is more complex than this; and he veers like
the wind. He has, moreover, the "horrible Imaginings" and
"sorryest Fancies" of the mercurial man; and his wife declares
that these are "a thing of Custome" with him, and he is "often
thus," and has been "from his youth." At night, he has "terrible dreams" and "restless ecstasy." He is most susceptible to
the suggestions of the Wierd Sisters, and even seeks them to
find out "By the worst meanes, the worst." The mercurial
complexion was "proud," and Macbeth has "Vaulting Ambition" that urged him to the crown and so to all his evil deeds.
He is the perfect royal misfit; Richard was born to the throne,
and so should have been truly royal, but his complexion belied
his blood; Macbeth was not to the manner born, and showed
it in his mercurial temperament.[16]

This mercurial temper, because it was yielding and could
be crafty, sometimes had its advantages even in high places;
provided that one could somewhat control one's shifting
moods. Such was Cleopatra, who, womanlike, founded her
power on her weakness. According to Plutarch, she charmed
by "her beautie, the excellent grace and sweetenesse of her
tongue." She was expert in devising "newe delights" for Antony; but she was shrewd in judging men, and did not hesitate
sometimes to taunt and mock him. This Cleopatra suggests
the mercurial entertainer Feste; and Shakespeare conceived her
along the same mercurial lines. She at once loves Antony,
amuses him, and betrays him. She flees at Actium and sends
secret messengers to Octavius, and yet she mourns for her
lover with a depth of feeling that cannot be quite insincere.
Shakespeare's picture of her actions and her character closely
follows Plutarch, but the dramatist seems to emphasize even

[15] L. B. Campbell, *Shakespeare's Tragic Heroes* (Cambridge, 1930), pp. 208 *et
seq.*

[16] See the present writer, "Macbeth, 'Infirme of Purpose,' " *Bull. Hist. Med.*, X,
16 *et seq.*

more than did the biographer her mercurial complexion. When she loved Julius Caesar, she was "greene in iudgement, cold in blood"; but now she is "cunning past mans thought." Her recipe for managing Antony is that of a sophisticated grownup with a child; and the Romans must have seemed childlike barbarians to the Orientals of that age: she gives Antony endless change; and indeed, Enobarbus described her rightly in the oft-quoted lines:

> Age cannot wither, nor custome stale
> Her infinite variety.

Of Antony, she herself declares:

> I laught him out of patience: and that night
> I laught him into patience, and next morne,
> Ere the ninth houre, I drunke him to his bed:
> Then put my Tires and Mantles on him, whilst
> I wore his Sword Phillippian.

With all her emotional violence, she is shrewd, and recognizes the dissembling of Octavius; and, at the end, she even draws from him a grudging word of praise, when he sees her dead and calls her "Bravest at the last." How far she controlled the "infinite variety" of her mercurial temper, how far it was feminine instinct, and how far mere chance is hard to say; but is not this the ageless enigma of womankind?

The mercurial complexion, often brilliant and always undependable, forms a sharp contrast to that other combination of humors, the perfectly balanced character, which was reliable but too sober to be brilliant: Cleopatra and Horatio are indeed at opposite poles of human personality; and, somewhat like Cleopatra in scintillant instability are little Moth in *Love's Labour's*, Mercutio, Puck, and Feste. Lacking the brilliance, but still unstable, are Richard II, Julius Caesar, and Macbeth. In a purely ornamental social place, like Feste's, such personalities shone; but, for the demands of serious life, the somewhat drab Horatio was a stauncher pillar than Richard or Macbeth or even the glamorous and wily Cleopatra.

CHAPTER VII

COUNTERFEIT HUMORS

Shakespeare's characterization is too close to life to be as simple as the preceding chapters might imply. Ben Jonson delineates a whole play-full of persons, each one moved throughout the action, like Richard III or Cassio, by a single-humor that is obviously their nature's livery and fortune's star; and Ben Jonson's humors, therefore, are often oversimple and somewhat artificial. The major characters, however, of Shakespeare's greater plays commonly follow more complex patterns, and transcend such elementary types. Indeed, in life, one is not always dull or brilliant or malevolent or genial, but varies with the company and the occasion; and, just as a multiplicity of factors reflect in our passing moods and manners, so under Shakespeare's magic touch, his full-length portraits bend and are bent through the influence of passing episode, and turn to the audience shifting facets of their personalities. Thus in the course of a play, the humor of a character may actually change; or a character, as in life, may have reason to conceal its true nature, perhaps by more or less conscious deception, or by those small hypocrisies of politeness that keep society running smoothly, or by the monumental shams of a nation-shaking conspiracy. These personal changes and disguises so common in the complex tissue of real life and so finely reflected in the plays, doubtless in part account for scholars' previous neglect of the humors in Shakespeare's technique of characterization. Everyone has recognized that back in the 1590's, Ben Jonson was writing comedies of humor; and, in Shakespeare's plays, everyone has recognized scores, not to say hundreds, of allusions to matters humoral, alchemical, and astrological; but the tissue of characterization that the master wove from these fine threads was so intricate in texture and design that editors have been somewhat lost in its detail and appreciative critics have overlooked these elements in the characters. Indeed, even Professor Hardin Craig, who has long labored in the field of Renaissance science and who has both taught and edited Shakespeare, only a few years since declared: "Shakespeare, for the most part, stayed off the shaky ground of unsubstantial science and pseudo-science. . . ."[1]

The present chapter proposes to discuss examples of humors more or less consciously assumed or counterfeited by Shakespeare's characters. Their motive is sometimes self-protection; for one who really understands the character of another, as Iago did Cassio's, can play on that other what tune he pleases; and so prudence dictates that a man conceal himself behind some façade acceptable to his little world but not too candidly revealing. Sometimes one's occupation, as in the cases of Falstaff and of Viola, may require a humor different from one's innate character; or the situation of the moment, as in the case of the exiled Malcolm when first he meets Macduff, may demand a stratagem of deception. Sometimes, the motive is hypocrisy on a grand scale with national consequences, as with Goneril and Regan in the first scene of *Lear,* or with the dissembling Edmund. Perhaps the old play, *The Taming of a Shrew,* in which Kate merely assumes her choler, gave Shakespeare the hint for this dramatic motive: in either case, his dramas present examples of all the humors assumed for one reason or another, with much or little success; and the present study will take up severally the pretense of each of the four and also of the mercurial complexion.

Melancholic persons, being given to trickery and deceit, were particularly apt at assuming a false appearance; and the humor they often chose was the direct opposite of themselves, the genial, open, sanguine disposition, calculated to allay the suspicions of their dupes: so it is with Richard III and with

[1] H. Craig, *The Enchanted Glass* (New York, 1936), p. 82.

Edmund, who are both by nature melancholy, and with Iago, who, as an old soldier, suffered from the almost-as-dangerous complaint of martial choler; so with Viola, who, as a woman, should be phlegmatic, but can play the courtier to Orsino's sir and to Olivia's madam with such swift and marked success. For her, the sanguine humor has become almost second nature, doubtless because of some natural inclination toward it; but Macbeth, even at his Lady's urging, cannot "look like the innocent flower," and flees from the banquet with Duncan. Richard and Edmund, Iago and Macbeth, plot to advance their evil interests and lure their enemies to ruin; and Viola plots to lure the love-enraptured Duke into the toils of marriage with herself. Richard is not quite convincing, especially in his wooing of Lady Anne; and Viola must have been unbelievably entrancing to win the favor of the Duke and the love of his Lady at first sight: in history-plays and comedy, such doubtful motivation might be overlooked; but high tragedy requires a more convincing disguise of friendliness and charm; and Shakespeare rose to the occasion.

Iago, for all Professor Stoll's objections,[2] is a convincing deceiver: in the first place, his "honest" past—which we must take for granted, or call his commander a fool[3]—had prepared Othello and Desdemona to expect in him no guile; in the second place, he generally tries to act, not the sanguine courtier, for which he had few accomplishments and graces, but the blunt choleric soldier, which, on the whole he really was. His chief excursion into courtliness appears when first Desdemona lands in Cyprus and he tries to while away her anxious tedium until Othello arrives, by partaking in an extempore *conversazione* on Woman and her virtue.[3a] His wit is a bit too cynical and heavy; but cynicism on this set topic was an accepted attitude, supported by the Christian dogmas of Mother Eve and the "weaker vessel." With consummate realism, Shakespeare makes Iago a poor player of the part; and the polished Cassio

[2] E. E. Stoll, *Othello, an Historical and Comparative Study* (Minneapolis, Minn., 1915).

[3] See the present writer, " 'Honest Iago,' " *PMLA*, XLVI, 724 *et seq.*

[3a] See the present writer, "Shakespeare and the *Conversazione*," about to appear.

has to excuse him and assure Desdemona that she will relish him more in the soldier than in the scholar. The very fact that Iago cannot bandy cavalier compliment would, moreover, make him seem to Desdemona and Cassio all the more straightforward and reliable. Thus Iago, like a modern actor who can only play himself, takes his own choleric bluntness as his main disguise, and in this instance of attempted court-liness can afford to fail; and, indeed, it would seem that Shake-speare early in the play gives us this instance of Iago's poor ability as an actor to show that in the main he is simply behaving in character as a normal petty officer of the age. Indeed, he is not capable of the Machiavellian guile that modern critics have imputed to him.

Old Gloucester at the very beginning of *Lear* introduces his illegitimate son Edmund as just returned from an education in foreign parts; and this traveled youth should be played as a past master in exotic elegance so combined with an affected modesty as to charm the rough nobility of a barbarous age— courtiers like his father and old Kent and even more the two cormorant duchesses, daughters of the half-abdicated King. In fact, the two latter shortly dote on him in defiance of decency and legal wedlock. His insinuating polish should contrast with the surrounding coarse barbarity; for he is point device the very man. He is schooled in the fine arts of Italianate deceit; he can forge a letter, lie convincingly, smile where he hates, and make love where he has no love—all this for no compelling motives like Iago's, but for a vague ambition, a hatred of mankind, and a natural taste for evil as pure and undisguised to his own conscience as that of Richard III. Under absolute monarchies such as flourished in the Renais-sance, no figure is more reviled than that of the court-flatterer who deceives the royal ear and so poisons the body politic at its very head;[4] and Edmund is the cunning flatterer raised to proportions of heroic evil. The sanguine temper, in short, is not only the temper of good men like Duncan who are easily

[4] See the present writer, "Flattery, a Shakespearean Tragic Theme," *PQ*, XVII, 240 *et seq.*

deceived, but also the assumed disguise of evil men, choleric
or melancholy, who aim to deceive others and commonly
succeed.

The phlegmatic cast of character was thought natural to
fools and women and children; and women, in their efforts,
comic or serious, to catch the desired husband were likely in
Elizabethan times to assume a passive, generally phlegmatic
role; for most Elizabethan men feared above all the independent woman, and ecclesiastical authority was utterly against
her. Even a rich and titled heiress like Olivia did not too
openly flout Dame Grundy in choosing a husband for herself
—a husband whom she intended to cherish but not obey; and,
all the more, a younger daughter like Bianca in *The Taming
of the Shrew,* who suffered under her father's ruling that the
elder must marry first, was obliged, with this overwhelming
disadvantage, to exercise every care to attract the timorous
suitor. The downright violence of her sister Kate gave her
the obvious cue of maidenly and coy retirement; and coy she
was, and sweetly helpless and quite fragile, until she had
passed the critical moment at the altar: then she soon let her
husband know how much she would obey him. In short, as
the last act shows, Bianca is actually as self-willed, if not as
openly choleric, as Katherine, but she can restrain herself for
the nonce to win a necessary point. Of course, Goneril and
Regan are even better examples. Their deception is so gross
and palpable, indeed so rank in nature, that Lear's acceptance
of it for true pay points plainly to his own senility. They
caricature courtly compliment into grotesquerie—even more
than Lady Macbeth when she greets Duncan—and all three
use the same mathematical hyperboles. Both Lear and Duncan are so gullible, the one by senility, the other by his sanguine humor, that Shakespeare did not need to give subtlety
to their deceivers.

Pretense of the phlegmatic humor belonged to women
rather than to men; for a man's personal reputation and indeed his very safety in that age of ready self-defense, would
hardly allow him to assume a temper that properly belonged

to dolts and children and women; and, when Prince Hal allows himself to sow his wild oats in Falstaff's doubtful company, he risks, not only Hotspur's contempt but also the loss of succession to the throne. Artists and poets were included in this humor; and the Fool in *Lear* might be thought of as assuming it. Certainly, most of the early fools were actual idiots; but Lear's jester is as shrewd as Olivia's Feste, and much more daring in his effort to make his master see his follies. The Fool is but a "boy," and so may be truly phlegmatic; but he is certainly not the idiot that his profession in that early age implied and that Lear chooses to think him. At his first entrance, he tells the all-too-candid Kent that one must "smile as the wind sits," or "wear my coxcomb"; and, despite his coxcomb, Lear is touchy at his quips, and cries, "Take heed sirrah; the whip," to which the Fool answers sententiously, "Truth is a dog must to kennel," and makes the old King a rhyme beginning:

> Have more than thou showest,
> Speak less then thou knowest . . .

With fine dramatic irony, Lear misses the point, and remarks, "This is nothing, fool." Goneril enters frowning, and her father begins to understand the wise Fool's chatter. Lear breaks with Goneril, and declares he will visit Regan; and the jester warns him that Regan will be no better, and tries to use the accepted treatment of diversion to combat melancholy and save his master's tottering wits; but his efforts are of less and less avail; and, when Lear finally raves, the Fool fades from the tragedy. Like the phlegmatic Benvolio in *Romeo and Juliet,* he tries to mitigate the full impact of catastrophe, but disappears before the final inevitable dissolution. Wisdom-under-the-guise-of-nonsense is the stock-in-trade of the Fool; only the license of a cap and bells, as Kent's fate showed, would permit the delivery of such warnings; and thus the Fool assumes a cloak of doltish phlegm, to try to counteract the cunningly assumed phlegmatic humor of the two ungrateful daughters; but the task is impossible.

The humor perhaps most commonly assumed was choler; for it accorded with the robustious temper of the age when a man's good right arm, dirk in belt and sword at side, took the place of regular police to maintain peace and order. Indeed, a reputation for bravery and swordmanship was necessary for safety on the streets. Thus Shallow[5] in his youth had played the bully buck in town, and thought he cut quite a figure. He had managed to gain admission to a second-rate Inn of Chancery, and there had imitated the worst taste in current fashions, played gay Lothario in houses of ill fame, was nicknamed "lusty Shallow" (or so he claimed in later years), and even fought a duel with a fruiterer behind Gray's Inn. (Imagine a real Elizabethan gentleman stooping to a fruiterer!) The names of Norfolk and the great John of Gaunt are on his tongue; but one fears that Falstaff is right in impugning both his courtly acquaintance and his choleric nature. Indeed, Falstaff himself should have been a good judge of counterfeit choler; for, almost habitually, he played that game himself. His poltroonery suggests that he is by nature phlegmatic; his age should be desiccating him to a feeble melancholy; and, despite his vast consumption of sweet wines,[6] he has enough *élan vital* only for buoyancy of wit and not for knightly action: in fact, in *Merry Wives,* he is himself a very Shallow, trying in vain to trade on a choleric manliness and a courtly connection that he does not possess. Nym is a more obvious example of the same.[7] He is always harping on his "humor," which he likes to have one think is for swordplay and heroic brawls; he speaks little, hoping that since he uses few words, people will take for granted his great deeds: in actual fact, however, he will not fight Pistol even when the latter cheats him of his ladylove and eight shillings, and soon makes a craven peace. Truly, the Falstaff group presents some edifying cases of simulated choleric valiance.

[5] See the present writer, "Robert Shallow Esq., J. P.," *Neuphil. Mitt.*, XXXVIII, 257 *et seq.*

[6] See Ruth E. Sims, "The Green Old Age of Falstaff," *Bull. Hist. Med.*, XIII, 144 *et seq.*

[7] See the present writer, "The Humor of Corporal Nym," *Sh. Assoc. Bull.*, XIII, 131 *et seq.*

Choler, however, might be assumed for higher purposes as in the examples of Petruchio and, on occasion, Prospero. Petruchio was a real upstanding fellow, not afraid of woman or devil or even of the two combined. Like a proper Renaissance youth, he had been on his travels and had his fling; and now he is ready to settle down and do his duty by the family and its retainers and hangers-on by getting a legitimate son and heir and so assuring the future of his great and ancient House. His actual bleak establishment off in the country suggests a sparsity of cash—a common complaint of Elizabethan county families—and there is certainly a sparsity of comfort. How could the bold Petruchio do better than marry the well-dowered daughter of the affluent and urbane Batista? Kate could stand the hardships of country life: in fact, country life was just the right abrasive to polish this very rough but brilliant diamond. Petruchio is a bit of a psychologist; and, as a virile youth, he doubtless has by nature something of the choleric about him, so that it was not too hard, especially with the help of muscadel, to give free rein to this humor and outface Kate herself. He is truculent and irascible beyond all reason. He glares and bawls and curses, and does it all (he shouts) out of regard for her: no water is good enough for her to wash in, and so, though she is begrimed with slime and mud, this finical city wife must still go dirty; no bed is good enough, and so she stays up all her marriage-night; no food is good enough, and so she starves. "Thus," says the husband in soliloquy, "have I politicly begun my reign"—not alone curing his wife's choler, but also, by the way, making it clear to his slack household that he has learned on his travels how a household should be run and so will not put up with their old sloppy ways. He watches narrowly the effects on Kate of his psychotherapy; and then he'll "rail and bawl," for "This is a way to kill a wife with kindness" and "curb her mad and headstrong [choleric] humor." Clearly, Petruchio is acting a "politic" part, and much of his mighty choler is a calculated pious fraud.[8]

[8] See the present writer, " 'Kate the Curst,' " *Jour. Nerv. Ment. Dis.*, LXXXIX, 759 *et seq.*

Prospero assumes choler, but more gently and for gentler purposes. The old magician knows that the course of true love must not run too smooth; and, furthermore, he wants to test this young Prince Ferdinand, who might indeed inherit some of his father's unsavory qualities. The innocent and admirable Miranda deserves the best of husbands, and Prospero proposes to make sure. Ferdinand is properly wrecked by the conjured-up storm; he is separated from the others, and led by Ariel to the vicinity of Prospero's cave, where Miranda may regard him and fall in love as her father planned. Prospero astutely feeds this love by treating the Prince rudely, binding him in enchantment, and forcing him to the menial task of carrying logs. Of course, Miranda, who at first mistook this "brave form" for a "spirit," is outraged, and therefore sympathetic, and therefore more and more in love. Of course, the Prince also is delighted, and, from the desolation of his late bereavements and his present durance, looks not only with favor but with fervor on Miranda. Indeed, there had been danger that he would look down on her rural naïveté from his princely height, and possibly, like Caliban, contemplate something less than marriage. All this, of course, Prospero means to circumvent; and so he makes the courtship "uneasy" and rigorous "lest too light winning Make the prize too light." He warms to the working of his benign stratagem; with his tongue in his cheek, he calls Ferdinand a "traitor" and his daughter a "foolish wench"; and, while he chaperones unseen, he lets the two steal some brief talk together. The delicate Miranda soon offers to help carry logs; the Prince calls her "most dear mistress" and a "precious creature"; and this success sets Prospero rejoicing like the fond parents in Rostand's *Les Romanesques,* who used similar means to a like happy end. Thus Prospero, like Petruchio, assumes a choler though he has it not, for the good purposes of a comic resolution. Counterfeit choler, in short, would seem to be the temper of soldiers less given to arms than soldiering and on occasion to psychological practitioners in some worthy cause.

Sometimes even the dangerous humor melancholy was likewise counterfeited in good cause. Hamlet pretends that his actual sorrow at his father's death is so great as to produce a melancholy madness; and he pretends so well that he deceives even the shrewd old Polonius and his own mother, who must have known his moods. This assumed madness at once saves him from answering inconvenient questions such as Claudius and his emissaries were wont to ask, and also gives him freer rein in speech and action to sound out others without rousing their suspicion. The device was an old one both in drama and in life; and the Elizabethans would at once have understood its purpose. Of course, his continued frustration as the play proceeds enhances his actual melancholy, so that in the final graveyard scene his bitter outbreak with Laertes is an authentic effect of the disease.[9] Olivia, likewise, experiences an actual melancholy from the deaths of two dear relatives, and augments and prolongs it to safeguard herself in a tricky situation; and she floods her chamber round with tears as a means of holding off the importunate Duke Orsino. Like Hamlet's, her humor was at first entirely authentic; but her badinage with Feste in the last scene of Act I shows that by then time had soothed her sorrow; and whatever melancholy she shows later either is assumed against Orsino, or arises from Viola's refusal of her proffered love. In her case, as in Hamlet's, the fact that the humor assumed is partly real makes her use of it the more natural and convincing.[10] Less real and therefore less convincing is Malcolm's assumption of an evil melancholy disposition when he meets Macduff in England. He asserts that in himself are found

> All the particulars of vice so grafted
> That, when they shall be open'd, black Macbeth
> Will seem as pure as snow, and the poor state
> Esteem him as a lamb, being compared
> With my confineless harms.

[9] See the present writer, The "Hamlet" of Shakespeare's Audience (Durham, N. C., 1938).

[10] See the present writer, The "Twelfth Night" of Shakespeare's Audience, chap. ix, about to appear.

Macduff is shocked; but Malcolm soon admits that he was only trying to find out whether the other was a spy sent by Macbeth. One of the oddest cases of false melancholy is that of Sly in the Induction of Shakespeare's *The Taming of the Shrew;* for he does not himself counterfeit the humor, but others insist, as part of the hoax they play on him, that for fifteen years he has been suffering from a melancholy lunacy, and has only just been "cured." The method of this cure, by music and mild diversions, accords with contemporary medical opinion.

One would hardly expect to find characters assuming the unstable mercurial temper; but one suspects that at times the jester Feste did so for professional reasons; and, indeed, Viola says as much of him:

> This fellow is wise enough to play the fool;
> And to do that well craves a kind of wit:
> He must observe their moods on whom he jests,
> The quality of persons, and the time,
> And, like a haggard, check at every feather
> That comes before his eye. This is a practice
> As full of labor as a wise man's art:
> For folly that he wisely shows is fit;
> But wise men, folly-fall'n, quite taint their wit.

Moreover, Cleopatra, who strives by her entrancing charms to save her crown and kingdom, seems also to augment her naturally mercurial temper; and she aims to hold her Roman lover by "infinite variety." She carefully sets the stage for their first meeting, then banquets him and plays his paramour, takes him afishing for a salted fish—until she quite bewilders the stern Roman, and makes him renounce wisdom and wife and country for her charms. She loves him, taunts him, plays with him, turns traitor in battle, and weeps over his loss, until she seems an enigma of contradictions. These pyrotechnics of caprice are not entirely mere accident or passing whim: like Feste, Cleopatra is an artist, an artist who must win or lose the highest stakes; and her love of Antony is indeed "a practice As full of labor as a wise man's art."

Examples can be found in which characters of almost every humor assume for convenience another of the humors; they assume the sanguine and the phlegmatic to flatter or deceive, the choleric and the melancholic as a means of self-protection. The most successful counterfeits are those in which the coin is partly gold, and the character, like Iago, is playing a part that is an actual facet of himself, though exaggerated and perhaps prolonged. The innate melancholy villains, like Richard III and Edmund, stretch our credulity a trifle further; for most of us do not believe in innate villainy, and we wonder also that their gulls do not shortly come to realize their true personalities. Shakespeare, indeed, shows his characters, like living men and women, striving to remake themselves at the behest of some ambition or some need. This is a portrayal of the conscious reaction of character to plot; the unconscious reaction in which events really change a personality will be treated in the following chapter.

CHAPTER VIII

CHANGING HUMORS

Environment is a fundamental conditioning factor in our lives; and what goes on around us more or less makes us what we are. Thus any dramatist who portrays events of magnitude and power must show some impress of such actions on the characters of those concerned; and therefore he cannot avoid some portrayal of character evolution. Sometimes this evolution may go on merely within a humor, as, for example, the growth of Coriolanus from choleric pride to treason and finally to ruin; but sometimes a person evolves from one humor to another, especially in the overwhelming progress of high tragedy. Although astrologers were inclined to stress the immutable power throughout one's life of the planet and the constellation of one's nativity, yet medical men, who emphasized rather the bodily fluids, were more willing to recognize these changes from one humor to another:

. . . sundry Physitiõs make no mo but foure differences, grounding their reasons (and not altogether vainly) y^t it is not possible (as Galene wytnesseth) that any temperature or distemperature can long continue alone and symple: For somuch as necessarilye it adopteth and taketh to it an other. For ye Hoate (consumynge & wastinge moysture) engendreth and bryngeth drynesse: Cold, consuming and wasting nothing, after a sorte encreaseth humour. Semblably, the Dry quality in those ages that a Creature groweth and encreaseth, maketh it hoater: but when it decreaseth and draweth towarde decay, it maketh colde and dryeth the solide partes of the body . . .[1]

[1] Lemnius, leaf 88 r.

Thus, we are told, untoward events, causing anxiety or fear, can change the individual's temper and even make the hair turn suddenly white.[2]

A number of Shakespeare's characters show clear traces of internal conflict of the humors, most notably King Claudius and Lady Macbeth. Though not a military hero like his brother, the Elder Hamlet, Claudius had served "against the French," and was accepted as a fit consort for the queen of a "warlike" state in the crisis of incipient rebellion.[3] He must, therefore, have been something of a soldier, and he certainly shows in his motives the vaulting pride and ambition of the choleric type; he had also the skill at deception and intrigue that went with melancholy; and, before the Queen and court and especially with Hamlet, he assumed a sanguine charm with such success that it cannot have been altogether against his nature. Outwardly, he played, as Macbeth indeed could not, the role of a good and gracious God-appointed king, at the very time that his soliloquies show his inmost soul racked with melancholy guilt and deep despair. He is one of the most complexly integrated characters in Shakespeare: strange irony that actors usually play him (as they do Iago) with the coarse mouthings and wooden gesture of the conventional heavy villain. In truth, he ranks with the most human of Shakespeare's creations, a man who sins greatly to satisfy a great desire, and yet would make only good come out of this great evil both for himself and others. Claudius is a magnificent actor in his manifold part, as husband, foster father, dastardly regicide and gracious king—in his early role of conciliating the young Prince, in the later play-scene when he conceals his guilt from all but Hamlet, and most of all in the final duel-scene when he watches the woman he loves so passionately die, and yet gives no outward sign: if it were not for soliloquy and aside, we should never guess the inner turmoils and torments between the conflicting humors that struggle for mastery in him. This struggle seems to continue through the

---

[2] *Ibid.*, leaf 92 r.

[3] See the present writer, *The "Hamlet" of Shakespeare's Audience* (Durham, N. C., 1938), chap. ix.

entire play, not resolved (as it is in Lear) by the final triumph of one element. It presents a strange condition of outward calm and inner violence that must have exhausted his physical powers and should at last have ended in consuming melancholy: indeed, the present author has sometimes wished that Shakespeare might have written another *Hamlet* with Claudius as the chief protagonist.

In Lady Macbeth, the struggle finds an inner resolution: as a woman, she must have been by nature more or less phlegmatic; her ambitions show her choleric; and her intrigues and madness point to a melancholy end. Shakespeare marks the first part of this struggle when she cries:

> Come, you spirits
> That tend on mortal thoughts, unsex me here,
> And fill me, from the crown to the toe, top-full
> Of direst cruelty! make thick my blood,
> Stop up the access and passage to remorse,
> That no compunctious visitings of nature
> Shake my fell purpose, nor keep peace between
> The effect and it! Come to my woman's breasts,
> And take my milk for gall . . .

Later she tells her husband that she would kill her child rather than give up the murder of Duncan, so utterly has she suppressed her womanly phlegm in choleric ambition. Her "fair" complexion and "little hand" suggest that she had by nature something of the choleric; and Macbeth appropriately declares:

> Bring forth men-children only;
> For thy undaunted mettle should compose
> Nothing but males.

Perhaps the summer season, as in *Romeo and Juliet,* had increased this choler in her; and, as with Falstaff, strong wine has helped to make her "bold"; but, even so, she has "visitings of nature"—womanly compunctions augmented by the likeness of Duncan to her father. She chid her husband, but she could not quite bring herself to do the deed; and, after the crisis is passed, she faints. The suppression of her proper woman's nature brings dreadful compensations. She is troubled by insomnia and terrible dreams; she walks in her sleep and reenacts the scenes of horror. At the banquet in honor of murdered Banquo, she shows, to be sure, some flicker of her former spirit, and saves Macbeth from imminent catastrophe; but her "heart is sorely charged"; she fears madness, and indeed is on the way to it. If Claudius was a supreme actor, she is truly a "poor player" at choleric "sound and fury," and finally wins, not the "solely sovereign sway and masterdom" that she had yearned for, but merely "nothing." She has not the strength of Claudius to endure a titanic inner struggle, and breaks under the strain.[4]

Sometimes a character runs through a recognized pattern of phases within the same humor, as when Othello turns from the choler that one might expect in a successful soldier to the raging choler of jealousy; and Coriolanus shows this evolution to the full: choleric pride, rage, treason, revenge, and ruin. But the present chapter is concerned with those figures who, like Lady Macbeth, are caught in the toils of circumstance and so are warped from their natural humor to another; and Shakespeare's more realistic plays of his middle period show a variety of examples.

The sanguine type, though fortunate and happy, easily turned to melancholy. This might happen, as with Romeo and Orsino, through unrequited love; but dire and undeserved misfortune might also bring it about, and Timon is a rather full case-history. According to the old tradition and to most Elizabethan versions, Timon was an unpleasing, not to say malignant, misanthrope soured by misfortune; but Shakespeare tries to make him a sympathetic figure who lost his wealth because he followed the ancient canons of liberality; and Timon's fall is made a reflection, not on Timon, but on the social and economic abuses that the government tolerated, abuses that bring the state to the verge of ruin.[5] "The Lord Timon" has a "good and gracious nature" which "outgoes the

---

[4] See the present writer, "Lady Macbeth," *Psychoan. Rev.,* XXVIII, 479 *et seq.*

[5] See the present writer, "The Theme of 'Timon of Athens,' " *MLR,* XXIX, 20 *et seq.*

very heart of kindness"; and public opinion honors him for a "right noble mind" and "illustrious virtue." Moreover, it is his "humor" that makes him so generous with his wealth; and this humor must be sanguine; but the senators who run the government are "cold" and melancholy, evil and pinching usurers. Timon suddenly learns that his riches are gone to pay extortionate creditors; none of his former friends will help him. He invites them to a feast of lukewarm water, and heaps insults on them, and then retires into the forests and renounces all human society. His soul is "distracted"; and "nought but humor sways him." He seems to turn first to choleric hate and fury, and this burns out his vital fluids to a deep melancholy that finally ends in madness and wicked suicide. Indeed, his "wits Are drown'd and lost in his calamities." Two of the characters attribute his final death to "melancholy."[6] Thus Timon's personality shows two transitions: the first, from the sanguine to the choleric, occasioned by the outward circumstance of loss of wealth and friends; the second, from choler to melancholy, occasioned by the inner violence of choler exhausting his vitality. The transitions show no particular struggle between the humors as in Lady Macbeth, but one state of mind grows naturally into the next in a reasonable and convincing evolution that does not seem so reasonable if one leaves out of account the psychology of humors.

The phlegmatic humor was too inert to be subject to great change; and yet one finds it changeable in Lady Macbeth and perhaps in a few other examples. As boys grew up, they naturally developed from the phlegmatic to the sanguine or the choleric; and Shakespeare shows us Macduff's little son who will not hear his father traduced as a traitor by a "shag-ear'd villain," and is stabbed to death for his courage. Falstaff's young page Robin also shows some signs of manly choler as he grows up in *Henry V* and fights for the King in France. In time of battle, to be sure, he wishes for "safety" and "an ale-house in London"; but, for all the sad and impotent con-

[6] See the present writer, "The Psychology of Shakespeare's Timon," *MLR,* XXXV, 521 *et seq.*

clusions of his roistering masters and companions, he is shown at the end still guarding the baggage with the other boys and sticking to his duty.[7]

Desdemona is perhaps the most psychologically difficult of all Shakespeare's heroines. She must have been brought up *une jeune fille comme il faut* according to the strict conventions of Venetian social usage; and yet she woos a husband under her father's nose and elopes with him without seeming to realize that such a disgrace to the family honor will kill the old man—as it does. Surely, this young lady shows a choleric independence quite brazed to the feelings of others. In the subsequent four acts, however, she becomes the submissive, almost childlike, wife of the jealous Othello, unable to understand his inner fury or rise to the occasion it induced. Perhaps Shakespeare thought of her as essentially phlegmatic, and "half the wooer" in the courtship only by some unexplained and transitory change in humor; but the present writer has elsewhere suggested that this curious contrast between the Desdemona of Act I and the Desdemona of the other acts arises from the fact that the former, since she belongs to a part of the play that Shakespeare added to his source in Cinthio, is a realistic Elizabethan young lady, whereas the Desdemona of the other acts, being based on the Italian story, is essentially the cloistered womanhood of Southern Europe;[8] and, furthermore, the *vraisemblance* required some assimilation of her character to the English noble ladies that the audience knew.

Bile was so strong a fluid that it burned out one's vital powers, especially in later years, and so might easily turn to melancholy; and thus it is in Lear, whom shock and passion and exposure in the storm finally reduce to madness.[9] By this same means of augmenting choler till it burns out its own fury, Petruchio cures Katherine, and reduces her to a proper womanly phlegm. Cleopatra's subduing of Antony's martial choler

[7] See the present writer, "Falstaff's Robin and Other Pages," *SP*, XXXVI, 476 *et seq.*

[8] See the present writer, "Desdemona," *Rev. Litt. Comp.*, XIII, 337 *et seq.*

[9] See the present writer, "The Old Age of King Lear," *JEGP*, XXXIX, 527 *et seq.*

to a luxurious phlegm by a round of exhausting pleasures shows her an even cleverer practical psychologist than Petruchio, whose heroic treatment was certainly less pleasing to the patient. With merrymaking day and night, with dalliance and taunting wiles, she wears out Antony, until he has no mind or thoughts left for his Roman wife or Roman politics, and makes so lasting an impression on him, that, even after he breaks away and seals a new alliance with Octavius and marries a new wife, he still must return to Egypt. This is truly an infatuation, and it changes his inner spirit from the soldier to the lover; and the crowding military losses of the latter acts are symbolic of the change. Indeed, his occupation's gone; and even at the beginning of the play,

> his captain's heart,
> Which in the scuffles of great fights hath burst
> The buckles on his breast, reneges all temper,
> And is become the bellows and the fan
> To cool a gipsy's lust.

And dying at the end, he has them bear him to her refuge to lay "the poor last" "Of many thousand kisses" on her lips. Cleopatra remoulded Antony to her heart's desire, and so brought both of them and the great realm of Egypt, to a tragic end.

The melancholic humor, belonging to old age and declining strength, was rarely a prelude to any other; and yet sometimes even this deadly temper gave away. Shylock as a Jew should be melancholy, and this would fit the covetous usurer.[10] He is "a stony adversary, an inhuman wretch Uncapable of pity." Even his daughter is "ashamed" of him; and his servant detests him as "the very devil incarnal." His wicked plot against the princely Antonio is a fit climax for such a character; and, when he has the merchant at his mercy, he is so intractable that the urgings of the Duke himself have no effect. He is a very wolf in sheep's clothing, and is appropriately referred to in the dialogue as a "wolf." It is his "humor,"

---

[10] See the present writer, "Usury in *The Merchant of Venice*," MP, XXXIII, 37 *et seq.*; and "The Psychology of Shylock," *Bull. Hist. Med.*, VIII, 643 *et seq.*

he says, to take Antonio's flesh; and he has a "lodged hate" against Antonio; and this "hate" suggests that the double misfortune of Jessica's elopement and the loss of his jewels has turned his natural melancholy to a violent inward choler. His whole purpose is to "plague" and "torture" Antonio; and his malice turns to incoherent "fury" so that in the scene with Tubal he cannot even follow a consecutive line of reason. He gloats over his "revenge"; and he swears an oath to heaven that he will not forego his bond. This vindictive temper finally defeats him; for, on these grounds, Portia, with good dramatic retribution, if poor law, rests her case. When his plots have been undone and he himself stands ruined, a suppliant at the bar, he begs them, "take my life," and when Antonio remits his share of the Jew's goods on condition of his conversion, and Shylock is—or at least says he is—"content," one wonders whether his choler, like Malvolio's at the end, is any whit the less.

Occasionally in Shakespeare, a thoroughly wicked person suddenly reforms, and so presumably changes from his evil melancholy or choler to some more beneficent complexion. Edmund, for instance, wishes to undo what he can of his misdeeds, but all in vain; and the usurping Duke in *As You Like It,* in the midst of his triumphant march against his good elder brother, is suddenly converted by a holy hermit to a realization of his sins. In neither of these cases, however, does Shakespeare's psychology keep pace with his plot: we accept what we are told for the sake of the play's conclusion, but wonder how the change could have been brought about. If Shylock, Edmund, and the usurping Duke finally escape from melancholy, poor old Falstaff struggles against it, but in vain. Like Claudius, he is one of the most complex characters in Shakespeare: he represents a transition from natural phlegm to the melancholy of white hair, under a cover of the assumed disguise of choler. He clung to life and the joy of living as he knew it; but at last he died with drawn face and babbling of green fields.

Shakespeare used the humors from his very first plays; but

his use of them grew more intricate as his characterization became more lifelike. In *Love's Labour's,* which is perhaps his earliest piece and is modeled on court-comedies of Lyly, he seems to borrow from Lyly the use of the humors for characterization.   At all events, almost all the characters, as in Lyly's *Endymion,* have clearly defined complexions: the King and Dumain are naturally sanguine; Biron and Longaville, naturally choleric under the gentle influence of the sun; and all four fail in their effort to lead the melancholy life of study. Biron is a particularly clear case; for he is "Full of comparisons and wounding flouts," and favors "fiery numbers" rather than "leaden contemplation."   Later, however, by a fine irony, he falls into love-melancholy; and, at the end, they are all left dangling and uncertain by the Princess and her ladies.   The "braggart" Spanish soldier, Don Armado, vaunts his "humor" as a sign of elegance and fashion; but it turns out that this humor is amorous "melancholy" for the not-too-elegant Jacquenetta, who seems quite willing to accept his love, and so should not inspire melancholy.   Constable Dull, with his "monster Ignorance" and the curate Nathaniel with his craven spirit, have lunar phlegm like Sir Andrew Aguecheek's; and the little page Moth seems to be mercurial.   Even as early as this play, therefore, Shakespeare shows, not only simple humors, but also something of disguise in Don Armado and something of a struggle in the King.   This is a great advance on Lyly's use of the simple humors; but the pastel shades in which the play is done are so evanescent that the details are obscured. Shortly after, however, in *Richard II,* he gives a full-length portrait of the complex mercurial type; in *The Taming of the Shrew,* he depicts one humor transformed into another and the whole method of the cure; and he shows in *Richard III* deception on a national scale.   Thus even as he entered on his period of realistic comedy of manners, he had mastered the technique of humoral characterization; and, in *Romeo and Juliet,* he even tried to write a whole tragedy motivated by astrology like the *Knight's Tale* of Chaucer.   This experiment was only a partial success, and he did not repeat it; but the humors as an explanation of character and motive he used to the very end: the present study has analyzed in some detail a score of major characters from his plays, and pointed out the humors of a hundred more; and, at the end of his literary career, *The Tempest* has a fine contrasting group (no less than in *Love's Labour's*) of sanguine, choleric, melancholy, and phlegmatic figures who speak and act according to their bodily fluids. Shakespeare's use of humoral terms and concepts is, in short, not only a major but also a permanent aspect of his dramatic art.

This subject is most difficult, and is beset with pitfalls; but, if the foregoing study has, on the whole, validity, then one may venture to appraise the importance of this approach to Shakespeare, and note what types of conclusion it may be expected to achieve. In the first place, it demonstrates the fundamental unity and verisimilitude of characters such as Macbeth and Cassio, some of whom have puzzled generations of Shakespeare critics. It has shown at least a sort of rationale behind the apparent incoherence of plot in *Romeo and Juliet,* with its half score of seeming coincidences. It gives a new meaning to such physical details as the "lean" Cassius and the "fat" Falstaff and Lady Macbeth's "little" hand, and relates Maria's wrenlike body and her tinkling wit. It gives to certain social details an added point: the Jewish usurer Shylock must be by nature melancholy and therefore probably bad; Lady Macbeth is a woman playing with choleric fire, and so breaks down and goes mad. Thus it explains many difficult cruces and *loci desperati* in the plays: the whole unpleasant situation in *The Taming of the Shrew,* the "merry war" of Beatrice and Benedick and its fortunate outcome, Olivia's independence and Cordelia's pert reply. It shows as strictly medical therapy the efforts of Benvolio to cure Romeo of love, and the efforts of the Fool to cure Lear's melancholy by diversion and of Cordelia to cure his madness by sleep and music, and the success of Orsino in curing himself by marrying Viola. Either by the cure or the growth of the condition, it explains the evolution of many characters: Shylock, Hamlet, Lear, Timon, Coriolanus, Antony. In short, this approach is necessary to the understanding not only of character but also of plot—for plot is merely what the characters do.

Perhaps this type of study is also valuable in shedding light on certain parallel problems: it tends, for instance, to answer Professor Stoll's contention that Shakespeare's characters are entirely and purely conventions of the stage with no modicum in them of Elizabethan life, and that the dramatist nowhere shows events molding and changing a personality. It supplements Professor Baldwin's study of the actors of Shakespeare's company in relation to various type-parts; for it suggests that these types—the choleric soldier, the sanguine courtier, and the rest—were largely humoral in their conception; furthermore, it suggests to writers on Shakespeare's life and personality and to students of his learning and the books he must have read, a facet of his varied interests that has previously been neglected. Most important of all, however, it is fundamental to any real study of the characters that Shakespeare created; and these characters are the most vital element in the plays he wrote; and these plays are the real reason why we are interested in the man, from whatever aspect we choose to study him and his vast accomplishment.

What was Shakespeare's attitude toward humankind, and how did he build his character-creations? The full answer is quite beyond the narrow scope of the present study; but perhaps one may hazard one or two suggestions. Free Will has always been a moot point in tragedy as well as in theology, ethics, and life. The protagonists of Greek drama—Oedipus, Antigone, Iphigenia—cannot avoid the crucial act that beckons to catastrophe: Fate and the gods decreed. Christian ethics elevated the human will; but astrology, more ancient than Christianity, still made men's lives the playthings of a superior force, the stars; and so, in Elizabethan times, astrology openly clashed with traditional Christian views. Humoral psychology is less deterministic and so more Christian; for a man might assume a humor he had not, or might mitigate one he had by avoiding things that would augment it: the choleric might eschew wine and fiery condiments, and try to guard against jealousy and violence; and obviously Cassio, when sober, has sufficiently overcome his natural choler to be quite a civilized Hotspur. Hamlet, in his melancholy, seeks restraint and balance in the companionship of Horatio. Orsino can, if he really wishes, cure his love-melancholy by marrying a more amenable lady; and Petruchio and Don Pedro and Prospero can even change the humor of others and so bring happiness from evil. Thus the humoral interpretation of Shakespeare's characters does not make them the mere wire-pulled automatons of Fate: within these humoral patterns of cause and consequence, they have, as we have in actual life, a certain freedom of choice and action, and so may mold themselves to approximate the balance of perfect health. Shakespeare, in short, is no scientific mechanist. A modern novelist in his characters may depict the operation of heredity or environment; but the operation of these forces does not necessarily preclude their own freedom of decision, for men can change environment and sometimes circumvent heredity; and Shakespeare's figures, likewise, are portrayed, not the mere slaves, like Jonson's, of their humor, but struggling or succumbing as men do in actual life—as masters or as servants of their tendencies innate at birth or acquired by profession, age or situation among their fellows. Thus, within the complex pattern of the humors, the dramatist shows the impress on human character of social environment and (if not of heredity)[11] at least of those astrological accidents of birth that somewhat took its place in Renaissance belief.

Perhaps from this examination of Shakespeare's use of the humors, one may risk a guess as to how he created some of his characters. From his sources, he took mainly plot; and motivation of this plot required for convincing realism certain traits of character for each act of a given figure. If all these required traits were obviously choleric, as in Kate or Hotspur, then it was necessary only to reinforce them with further choleric detail and choleric speech and "business" on the stage.

[11] See the present writer, The "Hamlet" of Shakespeare's Audience (Durham, N. C., 1938), pp. 67-68.

The result would be a consistent simple type. In short, the action must be motivated in the terms of Elizabethan psychological theory. Sometimes, as in Richard II, Brutus and Antony, the source implied a confusion of humors, or a humor that did not supply the required motivation and then Shakespeare had a problem of nice choice and adjustment. Sometimes, his theme required a type of character different from that which history or fiction gave him: thus he changed Duncan from a weak, phlegmatic king unfit to rule, to a sanguine monarch, possessor of all virtues but easily deceived; for his theme—the contrast of a good and rightful king with a bad usurper—demanded an admirable Duncan, who must be sanguine·or choleric, as a king should be. The choleric temper would make him too strong to be readily overthrown; and so the sanguine was the only possible psychology for Duncan. More complex are the cases where the impress of event required a character to change from one humor to another: here, as in Cassio's drunkenness and Lear's old age, the metamorphosis must appear by the recognized gradations; and, in the process of transition, each stage must be shown as the effect of some preceding situation or event that, according to humoral theory, would properly produce it: thus Cassio's drunken utterance must express the recognized phases of his increasing drunken choler; and Lear, as he suffers from mental shock and then physical exposure in the storm, must lose the power of his vital fluids, and waste away by degrees into a frenzied melancholy. So Shakespeare, within the complex pattern of humoral psychology, presents his characters, some simple, static types, some torn with tumultuous change; but, simple or complex, these figures, to be convincing, or even comprehensible, to his audience, had to be expressed in terms of the humoral psychology accepted by the age.

Each generation deposits a film of change upon the past, change of society, of language, and of thought; and, if we are to maintain that understanding of the past that differentiates us from the animals, then we must constantly remove this film, as one might polish a piece of fine old silver to renew its luster.

This is the task of scholarship, to keep our ancestral heritage vivid and bright before us so that we may learn from the wisdom of experience rather than merely trust to instinct like the animals. Not only is this true in political and economic history, but also in social history and in the allied histories of the arts and sciences—in medical and in literary history, for example; and each of these historical avenues into the past must be explored in relation to other avenues that cross it. Indeed, all the aspects of life in a given age more or less react on one another; and none can be truly understood without taking thought of the others that bear upon it. The past, therefore, should be explored down more than one converging road; and, though medicine and drama may at first glance seem unrelated, the need of the latter for psychological expression forges a major link; and thus contemporary medicine is one vista through which Shakespeare's characters can, and should, be viewed; for it is the way that the Elizabethans themselves viewed his vivid and complex creations. Seen from this angle, details of speech and action in the plays focus into a clearer relationship that reveals a greater unity of personality and a stronger nexus of motivation between character and plot. Thus the film with which time has overlaid the plays can somewhat be removed and something of their pristine life and meaning be restored; and something can be glimpsed even of Shakespeare's method as a creative artist: surely, all this is a major purpose of the honorable task that is the literary scholar's.

A SELECT LIST OF ELIZABETHAN
TREATISES AND HANDBOOKS
ON THE HUMORS

ADAMS, T. *Diseases of the Soule.* London, 1616. (Adams published some thirty volumes on religious subjects and brought out a collected edition in 1629.)

ANGLICUS, BARTHOLOMÆUS. *See* Batman, S.

ARCANDAM (pseud.). *The Most Excellent Booke of Dr. Arcandam,* tr. W. Warde. London, ?1562, 1592, 1626, 1630, 1634, 1637. (A very popular work according to L. B. Wright, *Middle-Class Culture in Elizabethan England,* Chapel Hill, N. C., 1935, p. 594.)

BARROUGH, P. *Method of Phisicke.* London, 1583, 1590, 1596, 1601, 1610, 1617, 1624, 1634, 1639. (See Wright, p. 586.)

Batman vppon Bartholome his Booke De Proprietatibus rerum. London, 1582, 1583, 1587. (See Wright, p. 552.)

BOAYSTUAU (also BOAISTUAU), P. *Theatrum Mundi,* tr. J. Alday. London, ?1566, 1574, 1581, 1587, 1595, 1615. (See Wright, p. 555.)

BOORDE, A. *Dyetary.* London, 1542, 1547, 1562, 1576. (Also ed. *EETS,* Ex. Ser. X.)

BRETON, N. *Fantastics.* London, 1626.

————. *Melancholicke Humours.* London, 1600. (Also ed. Harrison, 1929.)

BRIGHT, T. *Treatise of Melancholy.* London, 1586 (2 eds.), 1613. (See Wright, p. 589. There is also a recent facsimile edition.)

BULLEIN, W. *Bvlleins Bulwarke of defēce.* London, 1579 (2 eds.). (See Wright, pp. 574-575.)

BURTON, R. *The Anatomy of Melancholy.* Oxford, 1621, 1622, 1628, 1632, 1638.

CHARRON, P. *Of wisdome,* tr. S. Lennard. London, 1612 (3 eds.), 1630, 1640.

CLOWES, W. *Proved Practice of all Young Chirgeons.* London, 1588, 1591.

Coeffeteau, N. *Table of Humane Passions,* tr. E. Grimeston. London, 1621.

Cogan, T. *Hauen of Health.* London, 1584, 1588, 1589, 1596, 1605, 1612, 1636. (See Wright, p. 585.)

Cuffe, H. *The Differences of the Ages of Mans Life.* London, 1607, 1626, 1640.

Dariot, C. *Astrologicall Iudgement of the Starres,* tr. F. Wither. London, 1583, 1598. (See Wright, p. 585.)

Downame, J. *Spiritual Physicke.* London, 1600.

Elyot, Sir T. *Castel of Helth.* London, 1539, 1541 (4 eds.?), 1547, ?1559, ?1560, 1561, 1572, 1580 (2 eds.?), 1587, 1595, 1610. (See Wright, pp. 582-585.)

Fage, J. *Speculum Ægrotorum.* London, 1606.

Ferrand, J. Ἐρωτομανία, *or a Treatise of Love.* Oxford, 1640.

Fludd, R. *Metaphysica Physica atque Technica Historia.* Opphemi, 1617-1618.

Harvey, R. *Astrological Discourse.* London, 1582; 2d ed. with supplement, 1583.

Hill (also Hyll), T. *Art of Phisiognomy.* Appended to 2d ed. of *Contemplation of Mankinde.* London, 1613. (See Wright, pp. 565 *et seq.*)

———. *Schoole of Skil.* London, 1599. (See Wright, pp. 565 *et seq.*)

Huarte, J. *Examen de Ingenios,* tr. R. C[arew]. London, 1590, 1594, 1596, 1604, 1616. (See Wright, p. 105.)

de La Primaudaye, P. *French Academy,* tr. T. B. London, 1586, 1589, 1594, 1602, 1614. (See Wright, pp. 555-556.)

Laurentius, M. Andreas. *Discourse of the Preservation of the Sight,* tr. R. Surphlet. London, 1599. (Also ed. S. V. Larkey for Shakespeare Association, Oxford, 1938.)

Lemnius, L. *Touchstone of Complexions,* tr. T. Newton. London, 1565, 1576, 1581, 1591, 1633.

[M., I.] *General Practise of Medicine.* London, 1634.

de Mornay, P. *Antonius.* London, 1592, 1600, 1606, 1607. (See prefatory "Discourse.")

Moulton, T. *Myrrour or Glass of Health.* London, 1539. (The editions of this book have not been clearly differentiated, but Wright [p. 584] may be right in saying that there were fourteen down to 1580.)

NEWTON, T. *See* Lemnius, L.

OVERBURY, SIR T. *Characters.* London, 1614 (4 eds.), 1615, 1616
  (3 eds.), 1618, 1622, 1626, 1627, 1628, 1630, 1632, 1638.

PTOLEMY. *Tetrabiblos,* tr. Ashmand. London, 1827. Tr. in summary in 1532?, 1535?, 1540?.

SALERNO. *The Englishmans doctor. Or, the Schoole of Salerne,* tr.
  J. Harrington. London, 1607, 1608, 1609, 1617, 1624.

————. *Regimen Sanitatis Salerni,* tr. T. Paynell. London, 1528,
  1530, 1535, 1541, 1557, 1575, 1597, 1617, 1634. (See Wright,
  p. 583.)

VARCHI, B. *Blazon of Jealousie,* tr. R. Tofte. London, 1615.

VAUGHAN, W. *Directions for Health.* London, 1600, 1602, 1607,
  1612, 1617, 1626, 1633. (See Wright, pp. 587-588.)

VICARY, T. *Anatomie of mans body.* London, 1548, 1577, 1585,
  1586, 1587, 1596, 1613, 1626, 1633. (Also ed. *EETS,* Ex. Ser.,
  LIII, 188; see also Wright, p. 581.)

W[ALKINGTON], T. *Optick Glasse of Humors.* London, 1607,
  ?1631, 1639. (See Wright, p. 590.)

W[RIGHT], T. *Passions of the Minde.* London, 1601, 1604, 1620,
  1621, 1630. (See Wright, p. 589.)

INDEX